MIKE SCHMOKER

RESULTS
NOW

HOW WE CAN ACHIEVE UNPRECEDENTED
IMPROVEMENTS IN TEACHING AND LEARNING

Association for Supervision and Curriculum Development
Alexandria, Virginia USA

D0254183

Association for Supervision and Curriculum Development
1703 N. Beauregard St. • Alexandria, VA 22311-1714 USA
Phone: 800-933-2723 or 703-578-9600 • Fax: 703-575-5400
Web site: www.ascd.org • E-mail: member@ascd.org
Author guidelines: www.ascd.org/write

Gene R. Carter, *Executive Director;* Nancy Modrak, *Director of Publishing;* Julie Houtz, *Director of Book Editing & Production;* Deborah Siegel, *Project Manager;* Greer Beeken, *Graphic Designer;* Cynthia Stock, *Typesetter;* Dina Murray Seamon, *Production Specialist/Team Lead*

Copyright © 2006 by the Association for Supervision and Curriculum Development (ASCD). All rights reserved. No part of this publication may be reproduced or transmitted in any form or by any means, electronic or mechanical, including photocopy, recording, or any information storage and retrieval system, without permission from ASCD. Readers who wish to duplicate material copyrighted by ASCD may do so for a small fee by contacting the Copyright Clearance Center (CCC), 222 Rosewood Dr., Danvers, MA 01923, USA (phone: 978-750-8400; fax: 978-646-8600; Web: http://www.copyright.com). For requests to reprint rather than photocopy, contact ASCD's permissions office: 703-578-9600 or permissions@ascd.org.

Printed in the United States of America. Cover art copyright © 2006 by ASCD. ASCD publications present a variety of viewpoints. The views expressed or implied in this book should not be interpreted as official positions of the Association.

All Web links in this book are correct as of the publication date below but may have become inactive or otherwise modified since that time. If you notice a deactivated or changed link, please e-mail books@ascd.org with the words "Link Update" in the subject line. In your message, please specify the Web link, the book title, and the page number on which the link appears.

ASCD Member Book, No. FY06-08 (July 2006, PC). ASCD Member Books mail to Premium (P), Comprehensive (C), and Regular (R) members on this schedule: Jan., PC; Feb., P; Apr., PCR; May, P; July, PC; Aug., P; Sept., PCR; Nov., PC; Dec., P.

PAPERBACK ISBN-13: 978-1-4166-0358-0 ASCD product #106045
PAPERBACK ISBN-10: 1-4166-0358-1
Also available as an e-book through ebrary, netLibrary, and many online booksellers (see Books in Print for the ISBNs).

Quantity discounts for the paperback edition only: 10–49 copies, 10%; 50+ copies, 15%; for 1,000 or more copies, call 800-933-2723, ext. 5634, or 703-575-5634. For desk copies: member@ascd.org.

Library of Congress Cataloging-in-Publication Data

Schmoker, Michael J.
    Results now : how we can achieve unprecedented improvements in teaching
and learning / Mike Schmoker.
        p. cm.
    Includes bibliographical references and index.
    ISBN-13: 978-1-4166-0358-0 (pbk. : alk. paper)
    ISBN-10: 1-4166-0358-1 (pbk. : alk. paper) 1. School improvement
programs—United States. 2. Educational change—United States. 3.
Education—Aims and objectives—United States. I. Title.

    LB2822.82.S356 2006
    371.2'03—dc22

                                                            2006004771

15 14 13 12 11 10 09 08 07 06   1 2 3 4 5 6 7 8 9 10 11 12

• • •

Leadership is about vision. But leadership is equally
about creating a climate where the truth is heard
and the brutal facts confronted.

—Jim Collins in *Good to Great*

At a time when Americans seek strength in their leaders,
[we] should find the strength to speak hard truths about
our schools and support essential changes.

—Robert Gordon, education advisor to John Kerry

• • •

RESULTS NOW

HOW WE CAN ACHIEVE UNPRECEDENTED
IMPROVEMENTS IN TEACHING AND LEARNING

Acknowledgments

First, special thanks to the many audiences of educators whose consistently positive response to the hard truths included here convinced me that we were ready for the message contained in this book. Doug Reeves, Kim Marshall, and Rick DuFour gave me excellent, invaluable advice on early drafts and title ideas. I continue to appreciate Kim Marshall's superb summaries and opinions of the best educational writing in his weekly "Marshall Memo."

Several people have had an especially profound influence on my thinking both recently and over the years: Richard Allington, Rick and Becky DuFour, Bob Eaker, Richard Elmore, Michael Fullan, Carl Glickman, Kati Haycock, Frederick Hess, Judith Little, Kim Marshall, Bob Marzano, Jay McTighe, Doug Reeves, Ted Sizer, Dennis Sparks, Rick Stiggins, and Grant Wiggins. The influence of their work and thought on my own thinking has been immeasurable.

The staff at ASCD was, as always, wonderful—Nancy Modrak, Scott Willis, Julie Houtz, and Carolyn Pool. Deborah Siegel and Terrey Hatcher Quindlen guided the editing of this project with grace and efficiency. There are lots of people who made indirect but valuable contributions: James Bartell, Karen Epperly, Mike Malone, and the staff at Late for the Train coffee bar in Flagstaff, Arizona.

Finally, I owe so much, in every way, to my wife, Cheryl, and my daughters, Michelle and Megan.

Introduction

The Brutal Facts About Instruction and Its Supervision

We have operated under the BIG LIE for too long.
>—Loren Penman, a Pennsylvania school administrator

Effective teaching is quite different from the teaching that is typically found in most classrooms.
>—Allen Odden and Carolyn Kelley

Improvement "takes recognition of and moral outrage at ineffective practices."
>—Roland Barth

We must overcome the awful inertia of past decades.
>—Michael Fullan

Having an above average teacher for five years running can completely close the average gap between low-income students and others.
>—John Kain and Eric Hanushek

The question is not, Is it possible to educate all children well? but rather, Do we want to do it badly enough?
>—Deborah Meier

Place a good person in a bad system, and the system will win every time.
>—Seymour Sarason

The Opportunity

Imagine a time in the near future . . . when people speak matter-of-factly about how dropout rates and the achievement gap are inexorably shrinking, when record numbers of students are entering college, and when professors are noticing how much more intellectually fit each year's freshmen have become. Imagine palpable, irrepressible hope emerging in our poor and urban schools.

*All of these improvements result from a new candor that has emerged in education and a willingness to see that historic improvement isn't about "reform" but something much simpler: a tough, honest self-examination of the prevailing culture and practices of public schools, and a dramatic turn toward a singular and straightforward **focus on instruction.***

This book makes a radical claim: We have an opportunity to blow the lid off school attainment, dramatically and swiftly reduce the achievement gap, and enhance the "life chances" of all children, regardless of their social or economic circumstances. We have an opportunity to create schools better than anything we've ever seen or imagined. Higher test scores would only be a side-benefit of this transformation. Indeed, state assessments themselves would have to be significantly revised to adjust to this explosion in effectiveness, especially with respect to higher-order thinking and critical reasoning.

This is not a pipedream; we have clear evidence of this opportunity. Our schools continue to perform at current levels even though close studies of classroom practice over many years have revealed that most—though not all—instruction is mediocre or worse, as noted by Goodlad and Sizer (cited in Odden & Kelley, 2002), Elmore (2000), and the Learning 24/7 study (2005). For me, the most promising sign that these developments could transpire is that during my discussions and presentations over the last few years, *educators in overwhelming majorities have agreed that there is indeed a yawning gap between the most well-known, incontestably essential practices and the reality of most classrooms.* This gap persists despite the hard, often heroic work done by many teachers and administrators. To this majority of educators, for their candor and courage, I dedicate this book.

There are signs that we are making slow yet uneven progress, especially in the early grades (Murray, 2005). The advances predicted here would build on this progress, in a dramatic and swift fashion. We would achieve these results by addressing the monumental gap between common and effective teaching practices, and between typical and effective instructional supervision.

Jim Collins in *Good to Great* has famously urged organizations to see that the first difficult step toward improvement is to "confront the brutal facts" about themselves (2001a, p. 65). A rising chorus of voices is asking us to recognize that the brutal facts about teaching and its supervision are the way up and out of mediocrity. Robert Gordon, education advisor to John Kerry, pleads passionately for us to recognize that if we rectify our most glaring and manifest shortcomings, then we can achieve a social miracle. We can have an America where

> birth doesn't dictate destiny. Nothing offends democratic ideals more than the fact that a typical African American 12th grader reads at the same level as a typical middle-class or white 8th grader. Nothing is a greater threat to middle-class prosperity than mediocre schools. (2005, p. 24)

Gordon believes that we will move beyond mediocrity only by being much harder on ourselves and by "demanding educational *results*" from a system that could deliver them at far higher levels than we have wanted to admit (2005, p. 25). As we'll see, the performance of certain teachers, schools, and entire states proves this conclusively. Their accomplishments demonstrate that we haven't even begun to tap the enormous potential for dramatically better schools.

Are we up to this encounter and the changes it will require? Frederick Hess isn't so sure. He tells us that our public schools are characterized by a "culture of incompetence" (2004, p. 5). He believes that 20 years of reform, "staff development," training, and consultant visits reveal that draconian adjustments must be forced on the current system for it to improve. How valid a response can we muster against this argument?

Prominent voices from every camp are calling us to see schools as they are, to reckon, at last, with the unfortunate state into which teaching and its supervision have devolved. The path to improvement can begin only when we take seriously Michael Fullan's call to address, at long last, "the awful inertia of past decades" (2005, p. 32).

From Brutal Facts to World-Class Schools

This encounter with the brutal facts is the surest, fastest path to creating the best schools we've ever had. The challenge of writing this book is that the opportunity could be lost in the critique. That would be a shame, because a close look at these facts only reveals how close we are to better schools: the changes that will have the most impact on student learning require only reasonable efforts and adjustment, not more time. As Collins writes, greatness can be achieved "without increasing the number of hours we work" (2001b, p. 104).

Perhaps our chief obstacle is the prevailing perception that because most educators work hard and with dedication, we are within reason doing most of what's necessary for good schools. This is simply not the case. The system itself has prevented even the most talented and industrious among us from seeing this pronounced gap between poor and effective practices (Marzano, 2003, p. 23; Powell, Farrar & Cohen, 1985, p. 102; Lortie, 1975).

Swift, Systemic Change: A Precedent

There is a precedent for swift, significant transformation of an entire profession. In 1910, the medical profession had its honest encounter with the brutal facts. At that time, the most fundamental elements of professional practice were being routinely ignored. The problem wasn't a lack of knowledge or funding; the real problem was that there were no meaningful mechanisms for *monitoring and thus ensuring professional practice* and its improvement. As a result, there were countless, untold cases of unnecessary suffering, illness, and death.

Then, in 1910 Abraham Flexner was asked to visit hospitals and medical schools. Afterward, he wrote a frank report on the state of medical practice and medical education. The impact was seismic. As

Mark Clarfield writes, "it did not merely make waves. Rather, it produced a tsunami" of improvements that transformed medical practice forever (2004, p. 1).

It is critical for our profession, which has historically resented criticism, to know that Flexner was "not a man to mince words." He wrote with great candor about what he saw on his visits to medical schools and hospitals, deeming almost all of it "utterly hopeless" (Clarfield, 2004, p. 1).

Fortunately for all of us, the medical profession embraced rather than resisted these unpleasant but invaluable findings. Instead of discouraging the members of the medical community, these brutal facts opened their eyes to a historic opportunity. They realized that prodigious improvements were within their immediate reach. Hence the "tsunami" of benefits that ensued as the medical profession began to monitor and implement the most well-known and life-saving practices. Almost overnight, they closed what Pfeffer and Sutton (2000) would call the "knowing-doing gap." Some historians believe that Flexner reduced suffering and saved more lives than any man in history (Smith, 1987).

Educators are also in the life-saving business. Will we embrace the brutal facts? The intent of this book is to help awaken education to a similar opportunity. Be prepared: Section I contains a frank critique of typical schooling. The purpose here is not to discourage but to point to how existing funds of time, talent, and money are being misdirected. That is, they are being diverted from our greatest opportunity for better schools: *a simple, unswerving focus on those actions and arrangements that ensure effective, ever-improving instruction.*

Acting on What We Already Know

Happily, these historic advances can result largely from acting on what we already know (Pfeffer & Sutton, 2000). This approach is consistent with Carl Glickman's perennial assertion that the key components of effective schools are "not a mystery," even though they are exceedingly rare (2002, p. 4). Teachers themselves agree that these practices are widely known, that they can and should be carried out by people in any school and with current levels of funding—and that these practices can demonstrate how additional funding and higher teacher salaries could leverage even greater improvements (Hess, 2004; Fullan, 2005, p. 35; Miller, 2003).

In Chapters 5 and 6, we'll see how a commitment to such well-known practices will make its greatest mark in the areas most essential to school success, career advancement, and civic participation: higher levels of literacy and critical reasoning.

If we wish to resist the creeping dissolution of conventional public schools, we have to wake up to the fact that the experts are among us. The current system prevents these experts—practitioners—from acting on the best practices they already know and should be refining together continuously. In Chapter 8, we'll see how professional learning communities will allow us to make dramatic progress almost exclusively on the basis of in-house expertise.

Consider Bessemer Elementary School in Pueblo, Colorado. About 80 percent of students there are minorities who qualify for free or reduced-price lunches. Between 1997 and 1998, the number of students performing above standard in reading rose from 12 percent to 64 percent. In writing, achievement rose from 2 percent to 48 percent. And scores went up the next year as well—in all subjects. We're talking about the same teachers, same principal, same levels of funding—but leadership, at both the school and district level, underwent a sea change. The school set goals and identified areas of weakness. The staff made arrangements for teachers to work regularly in teams to share, prepare, assess, and then adjust their teaching on the basis of formative assessment results—a virtual definition of a true professional learning community (see Appendix B). Along with these steps, school leaders employed the talents of their best teachers—their in-house experts—to coach their colleagues toward better practices.

On the other end of the socioeconomic spectrum is affluent Adlai Stevenson High School—a one-school district in the Chicago area. Students and teachers there worked in the same team-based professional learning communities and benefited from the same honest, tough-minded leadership advocated here. They relied exclusively on in-house expertise as teams met, by course, to share and prepare lessons and units that they continuously improved on the basis of common, team-made assessment results. Over a 10-year period, under the leadership of Richard DuFour, Stevenson broke every achievement record on school, state, and college entrance exams. Advanced placement success increased by 800 percent (Schmoker, 2001b).

Such schools and districts point to the opportunity we have for vastly better schools, across the socioeconomic spectrum. Their success, like that of hundreds of other schools and a growing number of districts, underscores the importance of leadership that is exceptionally candid and built around self-managing teams (Schmoker 1999; Schmoker 2001b). But schools that function as professional learning communities are still in a distinct minority. If we truly desire better schools on a large scale, then we have to make these collaborative structures the norm—an expectation from the state, district, and school. Section III will make the case for the essential elements of professional learning communities. We'll see how they could lead to a renaissance in leadership at every level.

These few, simple structures and practices act magically on levels of achievement, because they directly affect the factor with the largest influence on learning: instruction.

Instruction: The #1 Factor in Achievement

Schools like Bessemer and Stevenson force us to confront the fact that the single greatest determinant of learning is not socioeconomic factors or funding levels. It is instruction. A bone-deep, institutional acknowledgment of this fact continues to elude us.

Let's look at just one teacher to see the full power of good instruction. As a high school English instructor, Sean Connors took a position in the poorest, lowest-achieving high school in his community, where writing scores were the lowest in town and well below the state average. I watched him teach. He was clear, organized, and effective. But more to the point, he did nothing unusual—nothing any teacher couldn't do or hasn't already learned. He was clear about which writing standards he expected students to learn on any particular day. He showed them samples of the kind of work he expected, and had students analyze and discuss the samples. He explained and modeled each specific skill—with students' involvement—on his overhead projector. He had students practice the new skills briefly in pairs, then individually while he circulated. He called on students randomly to share, so he could see if they were learning. Some educators call this a "check for understanding."

When Connors felt that students were ready, he assessed how well they had learned the new skill. There's nothing exotic in this approach. This simple lesson structure could be effectively repeated or varied for an endless number of standards, eventually saving precious preparation time.

But if you think such lessons are commonplace, think again. Yes, every element described above is absolutely basic; *every teacher has learned and can do such things at some level of proficiency.* But as we'll see in the next section, most teachers don't use these practices consistently. If more of them did, they would be getting results similar to Connors's: in one school year, scores at his school shot up by 26 points—from 59 percent to 85 percent—largely because of his efforts. There are many talented, hard-working teachers at his school. But it certainly looks as though they could learn from him (and he from them—bet on it). However, a brutal fact is that the culture of schools and school leadership militates against their ever learning from each other, despite the certain and enduring impact of such collaboration.

Why do such bizarre anomalies exist in our schools? Because, as we'll see in Section I, instruction isn't closely observed or supervised. As Robert Gordon points out, even in the age of accountability the current system "reinforces the irrelevance of achievement" (2005, p. 26). For all our reform, staff development, workshops, and conferences, very little close attention gets paid to actual teaching and its effectiveness. I see this indifference, this irrelevance, in schools where I've had an up-close look at classroom practice, where instruction is manifestly poor or mediocre. But almost nothing has changed—as long as that school hasn't been placed on some public list of "underperforming" schools.

Sadly, Connors's achievement wasn't noted or celebrated at the district or state level. Although hundreds of administrators expended thousands of hours in well-intended activities that school year, no one from the district or state education department ever so much as made a 5-minute phone call to congratulate Connors or to find out how he had achieved the largest writing gains in the state. No one asked or considered, "What can we learn from him? Can he do a presentation for other teachers?" This is what Gordon means by "the irrelevance of achievement." Connors left the district a year later.

It's About Teaching (Stupid)

Many will remember that Bill Clinton's first successful presidential campaign was focused on the idea that "it's about the economy, stupid." With due respect, we need to realize that "it's about teaching, stupid." Stories like Connors's and a pile of studies show how easily seduced we are by training or programs or products that divert us from a focus on sound (not perfect) teaching. Teaching needn't be exceptional to have a profound effect; continuous commonsense efforts to even roughly conform to effective practice and essential standards will make a life-changing difference for students across all socioeconomic levels.

The evidence is indisputable. Mortimore and Sammons (1987) found that teaching had 6 to 10 times as much impact on achievement as all other factors combined. Robert Marzano (2003) points to numerous studies demonstrating that two teachers working with the same socioeconomic population can achieve starkly different results on the same test: in one class, 27 percent of students will pass; in another, 72 percent—a life-changing difference. William Sanders, known for his "value-added" studies, found that just three years of effective teaching accounts on average for an improvement of 35 to 50 percentile points. That's in only three years. And the effects are enduring (Sanders & Horn, 1994). Eric Hanushek has found that five years of instruction from an above-average teacher could eliminate the achievement gap on some state assessments (Haycock, 2005). Indeed it has, and in entire districts (see Chapter 5 of Schmoker, 2001b). One recent study shows that the best teachers in a school have *six times as much impact* as the bottom third of teachers (Haycock & Huang, 2001). Researcher

Allen Odden and his colleague conclude that "improved classroom instruction is the prime factor to produce student achievement gains" (Odden & Wallace, 2003, p. 64).

The core argument of this book is that we know two things that constitute a truly historic opportunity for better schools:

1. Instruction itself has the largest influence on achievement (a fact still dimly acknowledged).

2. Most (though not all) instruction, despite our best intentions, is not effective but could improve significantly and swiftly through ordinary and accessible arrangements among teachers and administrators.

We have not done enough to clarify and broadcast these facts or the immense opportunity they so clearly afford us. To fully understand and appreciate this opportunity, we need to examine the institutional forces and traditions that prevent us from having an unimpeded view of our current reality and thus form a barrier to constructive improvement. Ingeniously, Richard Elmore calls this protective barrier "the buffer."

Section I

Reality and Illusion in Public Schools

In this section, we'll take a close look at the reality of schools—in the primary areas of supervision and instruction. An honest, unflinching examination of the current state of instruction, leadership, and the actual, taught curriculum points to an indisputably rich opportunity for educators and the students we serve.

In Chapter 1, we'll look at "the buffer" and how it prevents educators and communities alike from seeing instruction and supervision as it really is. The buffer keeps all of us from seeing how much better our schools could be.

In Chapter 2, we'll see how the buffer is both cause and effect of a hapless tradition of isolating educators from each other and from information that is essential to professional practice.

In Chapter 3, we'll see how the current system—a function of the buffer and teacher isolation, works to prevent leaders from having much influence on the quality of instruction.

In Chapter 4, an array of experts will weigh in on a crucial fact that hides one of our greatest opportunities: that what we teach varies markedly from what we think—or from any kind of common, high-quality curriculum.

At the end of this section, we'll see how real schools reveal that we need not be victims of these traditions. The way up and out is clear but will require courage, focus (like we've never had before) and a willingness to honestly confront the traditions and practices that have held us back for decades, with tragic consequences.

1 | The Buffer

How can anyone be sure that a particular set of new inputs will produce better outputs if we don't at least study what happens inside?

—Paul Black and Dylan Wiliam

The best explanation for why our schools aren't far more successful, intellectually engaging places is fairly simple: the most important people within and outside schools know very little about what actually goes on inside them.

One of the most compelling critiques of public schools you'll ever read is by Harvard's Richard Elmore: *Building a New Structure for School Leadership* (2000). In it, he describes how schools are protected by what he calls a "buffer." Think of it as a protective barrier that discourages and even punishes close, constructive scrutiny of instruction and the supervision of instruction. Its primary effect is to protect these two—the heart of schooling—"from outside inspection, interference, or disruption" (p. 6).

The buffer prevents communities and school boards from knowing what or how well teachers teach, and from knowing how well (or if at all) leaders supervise instruction. In turn, the buffer ensures that building principals know very little about what teachers teach, or how well they teach. And yet these are the primary factors that affect everything dear to us: learning, and equal educational and life opportunities. The buffer operates at several levels and with devastating consequences: it prevents teachers from knowing what or how well they or their colleagues teach. It deprives them of any meaningful frame of reference and discourages them from learning from each other.

The buffer, writ large, prevents anyone from seeing the details of schooling—good and bad—accurately. This barrier has led to the perception that instruction and supervision are conducted with relative effectiveness. It works so well that parents tend to give very high marks to their local schools. This rosy view promotes smooth relations among all entities. But make no mistake: this harmony exacts an enormous toll on the quality of schooling our children receive.

Elmore is not alone. A long line of critics have remarked on the crippling, if unintended, tradition of averting our eyes from what actually goes on in the classroom for the sake of harmony (Lortie, 1975; Little, 1987, 1990; Powell, Farrar, & Cohen, 1985). John Goodlad (1984) alludes to this in his classic study, *Behind the Classroom Door,* beyond which (as practitioners know) supervisors seldom pass. Judith Little has for years remarked on the private, protected world of teaching and recently lamented how the culture of "non-interference, privacy, and harmony" is precisely what prevents us from getting to the "tough work of school improvement" (Little, Gearhart, Curry, & Kafka, 2003, p. 190). This culture of privacy and non-interference is the best friend the status quo could ever ask for.

The Status Quo vs. an "Era of Unprecedented Effectiveness"

Recognizing the downside of this culture presents us with a breathtaking opportunity for improvement, not unlike what took place in the medical field. But grasping the opportunity, as Robert Marzano exhorts us, will require a courageous "commitment to change the status quo" (2003, p. 10). Like me, he's not sure we'll accept this challenge. But if we did, the rewards could be spectacular:

> K–12 education is on the brink of the best of times if we so choose
> . . . we can enter an *era of unprecedented effectiveness for the public
> practice of education*—one in which the vast majority of schools can

be highly effective in promoting student learning. (p.1) (emphasis added)

The buffer has prevented us from seeing the status quo clearly and vividly—from recognizing that the "vast majority of schools" simply do not provide effective instruction. This fact prevents us from entering this "era of unprecedented effectiveness."

The status quo gets enormous help from the machinery that creates the illusion of scrutiny and inspection—namely, teacher and administrative evaluations. Our annual surveys and "needs assessments" are followed by thick, detailed improvement plans, which are then followed by upbeat year-end reports from schools and districts. We've done all this for decades—without ever challenging the fundamentally sad state of instruction and supervision.

This machinery buffers us from seeing that the appearance of consistent, effective instruction and instructional supervision is illusory. A single classroom tour can destroy this illusion.

Beyond the Buffer: Looking in Classrooms

Over the years, I have persuaded teachers and administrators into doing something most don't do very often or with a clear focus: tour classrooms. I've done such tours in several states and in several hundred classrooms.

We're not looking for perfection. Nor are we looking for "bad" teachers. We're looking for schoolwide patterns with respect to two things:

- the general quality and substance of instruction
- students' attentiveness—are most of them on task?

Such a tour can spark an epiphany. An encounter with the alarming gap between reality and our assumptions about the general quality of classroom practice provides the essential starting point for improvement.

What do we see in the vast majority of classrooms? We find startling amounts of busy work, with no connection to important standards or a common curriculum. The system we place our teachers in, with its isolation and lack of constructive feedback or supervision, ensures that most of what we see is at odds with good practice.

In most cases, neither teachers nor students can articulate what they are supposed to be learning that day. They can describe only the activity or assignment, which is often chosen because it keeps kids occupied. Irrelevant worksheets and activities often predominate. Catching students learning the most vital reading and writing standards is heartbreakingly rare. And in defiance of what every educator has learned, there is a glaring absence of the most basic elements of an effective lesson: an essential, clearly defined learning objective followed by careful modeling or a clear sequence of steps, punctuated by efforts during the lesson to see how well students are paying attention or learning the material. In most classrooms, half or more of the students are clearly not engaged or paying attention.

Abetting this, and in violation of what almost every teacher knows, we continue to *call on that small minority of students who always raise their hands*—while the majority of kids tune out or chat quietly.

Finally, and with obvious consequences, an enormous proportion of daily lessons are simply never assessed—formally or informally. For the majority of lessons, no evidence exists by which a teacher could gauge or report on how well students are learning essential standards.

Such observations might seem discouraging, but in fact they point decisively to the opportunity to take immediate productive action. In Kerman, California, for example, a single one-hour tour was the catalyst for actions that resulted in dramatic, sustained gains in their elementary schools (Schmoker, 2001b, pp. 46-47).

Shock and Awe

There is always some initial shock, even denial, as the group hopes that the first few classrooms are an aberration. But they aren't. With each classroom visit, including return visits, the pattern is unmistakable. Almost every class reveals the instructional consequences of our historic failure to monitor or supervise instruction and arrange for teachers to work in teams so they can more effectively teach to clear, agreed-upon curriculum standards. For all we hear about how standards stifle "creativity," the very opposite is true. Where teachers deviate from common, essential standards, we see deadening, irrelevant activities proliferating. Years of isolation—from colleagues, from constructive supervision—account for this alarming gap between what we know and do. This gap can be seen in all schools, across the socioeconomic spectrum.

There are signs of modest, uneven improvements in light of the new state and federal accountabilities, but not on anything like the scale of what's possible. The "awful inertia" Fullan refers to continues to have a devastating impact on teaching and learning— and on students' lives.

A Matter of Record

If these observations seem distorted or subjective, don't believe them. Instead, conduct your own tours. Meanwhile, consider the following unfortunate realities, and remember to look for the enormous opportunities they represent.

• **Literacy.** Even in "good" schools, students read only a fraction of what they need for intellectual development. And they seldom write. Even fewer are ever truly shown how to read *critically* or to write *effectively*—the subject of Chapter 7 (Allington, 2001; Graff, 2003; Olson, 2005).

• **Curriculum.** In most schools, even the most talented, hardworking teachers do not typically follow a common curriculum. Despite slight improvements here, teachers continue to enter a system that allows them to teach largely what they want, regardless of importance or priority, at variance with any kind of coherent or agreed-upon curriculum (Popham, 2004; Hess, 2004; Berliner, 1984; Jacobs, 1997; Schmoker & Marzano, 1999).

• **Instructional Supervision.** In general, there is very little oversight of instruction that affects its quality. Administrators do not have any common, formal mechanisms to accurately gauge the content teachers are actually teaching or how effectively they are teaching it (Elmore, 2000; Marzano, 2003; Evans, 1996; Marshall, 2005).

• **Teamwork and Professional Learning Communities.** Unlike other professionals, and despite near-universal agreement on the importance of teaming, teachers do not work in teams. They do not prepare lessons and assessments together, and they do not test and refine their lessons regularly on the basis of assessment results (Wagner, 2004; Schmoker, 2005). In Chapter 8, we'll look at practical ways to rectify this situation.

A sobering recent study based on 1,500 classroom observations puts a fine point on these trends (Learning 24/7, 2005). If you care about student learning, these findings are chilling:

• Classrooms in which there was evidence of a clear learning objective: **4** percent

• Classrooms in which high-yield strategies were being used: **0.2** percent

• Classrooms in which there was evidence of higher-order thinking: **3** percent

• Classrooms in which students were either writing or using rubrics: **0**

• Classrooms in which fewer than one-half of students were paying attention: **85** percent

• Classrooms in which students were using worksheets (a bad sign): **52** percent

• Classrooms in which *noninstructional activities* were occurring: **35** percent

Such statistics point to how even fairly obvious actions could have an immediate and enormous impact on students and their levels of learning.

Improvement Is Not a Mystery

These brutal facts are roundly confirmed by our classroom tours. I have shared these findings with thousands of teachers, administrators, and even union heads from dozens of states. Overwhelmingly, they agree that the above observations are at least fairly accurate.

But they aren't inevitable. If anything, they point to clear, achievable opportunities for improvement. Look at where we're starting: surely even reasonable changes in supervision—in monitoring and feedback—would lead to dramatic reductions in the use of worksheets and noninstructional activities. We can just as surely increase, by large margins, instruction that includes the use of scoring rubrics, high-yield strategies, and higher-order thinking—all occurring in less than 3 percent of classrooms. As we'll see, improvements in these myriad areas will require only reasonable amounts of time and effort—far less if teachers work in teams.

These sad facts are the way out—the road to the best schools we've ever had. It is high time that state education departments and district leaders cease to be shy about such findings. They can "billboard" and broadcast these ripe opportunities prominently and passionately in schools, at district office and faculty meetings, at every state-level gathering, and in undergraduate and administrative preparation courses. We must turn the school improvement conversation on its head and admit at long last that, as Glickman points out, improvement "is not a mystery" (2002, p. 4).

We don't need more studies to begin this work with its predictable payoff. Unprecedented improvements will merely require that we reorient the heart, the time, and the energy we now invest in failed models and activities into those commonsense actions and practices by teachers and leaders that would address the deficiencies—the opportunities—just delineated.

Until we do, students will have to settle for the results we now get from our underachieving school system. As you look at the following results, consider the impact that the grave, unnecessary deficiencies just described—in curriculum, instruction, supervision, and student engagement—are having on the following dreary statistics. But also consider how simple, achievable changes in these areas could—and would—alter the status quo and transform the lives and hopes of tens of millions of children.

The Real-Life Impact on Students

If, as we've seen, teaching itself trumps all other factors affecting school performance, and if the shortcomings of most instruction are fairly observable and correctable—then consider the impact we could have on the following statistics:

- Thirty-eight percent of *all* 4th graders in the United States— almost 4 out of 10—read at the "below basic" level on the highly regarded National Assessment of Educational Progress (NAEP) (Haycock, 2005).

- By 8th grade, when patterns of success or failure are well-established, 43 percent of poor students are reading at the "below basic" level. In Math, 61 percent of black students and 53 percent of Latino students perform at the "below basic" level (Haycock, 2005).

- At the end of 12th grade, the average black or Latino student performs at about the same level as the average white 8th grader (Haycock, 2005).

- At a time when prospects for high school dropouts are plummeting, only 68 percent of students (not the previously presumed 85 percent) graduate from high school, and just over half of minority students graduate (Swanson, 2004).

- At a time when a college education is the ticket to success, only 7 percent of low-income students will earn a college degree (Haycock, 2005). About half of those who enter college "will never return for a second year" (Olson, 2005, p. 18).

- Lack of academic preparation, not financial need, is the chief reason for college failure. It should therefore disturb us that only 32 percent of our *college-bound* students are academically prepared for college (Cavanaugh, 2004a, p. 1). Of those wishing to attend college,

78 percent will struggle in writing, biology, and algebra (Cavanaugh, 2004b, p. 5). According to Naomi Housman, coordinator of the National High School Alliance, "Everyone is really beginning to realize the major leaks throughout the system" (Gervais, 2004, p. 15).

• According to the Organization for Economic Cooperation and Development, "Only 5 percent of Americans performed at the highest math level—compared with nearly a quarter of Finns, Koreans, Japanese, and Dutch" (Peterson, 2005, p. 3).

Stay with me here as we add one more crucial piece—the resounding evidence of what can be achieved in certain schools, districts, and entire states. This evidence vividly illustrates that these statistics are not even remotely inevitable, or due to socioeconomic or other factors that are beyond our control. Consider the following:

• In a number of states—including North Carolina, Ohio, and Illinois—a good number of the *highest-achieving* schools are not just poor, but *among the poorest* in the state. NAEP gains for minority students in these same states are about *three times* the gains for U.S. students overall.

• Only five years of above-average teaching could eliminate the achievement gap in some states (Kain & Hanushek, in Haycock, 2005).

• High-poverty, high-minority schools in New York City outperform their counterparts in Los Angeles and Washington, D.C., by *two full years.*

• Poor and minority students in some states outperform white, nonpoor students in several other states. For example, in Texas, black students perform better on the NAEP 8th grade writing assessment than white, nonpoor students in *seven other states.* In Virginia, Latinos perform better in 4th grade reading than white, nonpoor students in *17 states.* (Haycock, 2005)

Finally, Kati Haycock and research teams from the Washington-based Education Trust have found that there are "spectacularly wonderful teachers in every high-poverty school" (Haycock, 2005). We'll be meeting such teachers in later chapters. Their achievements point to the deep well of untapped, in-house expertise that can rescue our schools from mediocrity.

These observations and statistics, taken together, explode the old myths and excuses. They clearly show that our current results have to be a reflection of a school culture that, in too many cases, has an alarming tolerance for mediocre instruction, worksheets, and busy work—at the expense of effective, intellectually viable reading, writing, and learning activities.

Surely, we can make significant changes here, but not unless we're willing to take on this buffer, which prevents us from seeing these realities. At its heart is an unexamined addiction to privacy and isolation.

2 | Isolation
The Enemy of Improvement

The traditional school often functions as a collection of
independent contractors united by a common parking lot.

—Robert Eaker

How did the buffer become such an insidious feature of our schools?
It is important to see that it was given life and legitimacy on the basis
of the most superficially attractive logic and assumptions. These
assumptions took root long ago and are now part of the educational
landscape.

Back when, the sentimental notion emerged that teachers, left
to themselves, will automatically and consistently engage in effective
practices. After all, they are trained professionals who know how to
teach effectively, right? (This is partly true.) Therefore, the assumption
goes, teachers can—and should—be left alone. The buffer is thus justified on the basis of professionalism.

But this logic falls apart at several points. First, though most preparation programs ensure that teachers learn many essential instructional practices, these aren't reinforced or required in the schools
where they accept positions. If anything, school culture and supervision tend to ignore or divert teachers from implementing and continuously improving their mastery of effective instructional and assessment
practices. Every study shows that these practices are quite rare. What
teachers "know"—what they have learned—isn't developed or refined

on the job on the basis of collaborative, empirical processes. We don't commonly see teaching, followed by assessment, then adjustment to practice on the basis of assessment results. Some of the most incontrovertibly important practices aren't monitored or reinforced; they are allowed to recede into insignificance as poor or popular practices creep in to take their places.

Secondly, isolation masks the starkly different results achieved by different teachers. Without any point of comparison, the isolated teacher never has to confront the fact that (1) the teacher next door may be three times as effective as I am, or (2) much of my teaching is inferior (though parents and principals seem to like me as much—*or maybe more than*—that teacher next door).

The upshot: isolation ensures that highly unprofessional practices are tolerated and thus proliferate in the name of . . . professionalism. "What works" morphs easily into what feels good, or keeps kids occupied or "what I've always done and gotten good evaluations for." (As a teacher myself, I did plenty of silly things on this basis.)

As unpleasant as it is to write this, the above statistics make clear that we have created a system in which generations of talented, hardworking teachers have engaged in inferior practices without receiving feedback that would alert them to this fact.

Just Leave Me Alone and Let Me Teach!

Elmore tells us that the "educational change literature" is complicit here. It has bolstered such isolation with its "injunctions to respect the autonomy of teaching and the mystery of its fundamental practices—*hence the inviolability of individual teachers' choices about what to teach and how*" (2000, p. 7) (emphasis added). Doug Reeves writes trenchantly of how this misbegotten "inviolability" (combined with our history of ham-handed reforms) has teachers understandably pleading "Just leave me alone and let me teach!"(2001, p. 1).

But this is absurd, as Arthur Wise makes clear:

> Professionals do not work alone; they work in teams. Professionals begin their preparation in the university but do not arrive in the workplace ready to practice. They continue their preparation on

the job. In medical, legal, and architectural settings, services are provided by experienced and novice professionals working together to accomplish the goal—to heal the patient, win the lawsuit, plan the building. The team delivers the services... the novices learn by doing, with feedback and correction. (2004, p. 43)

This helps explain Kati Haycock's unpleasant finding: if we leave virtually every instructional choice up to individual teachers who work alone, then inferior practices will dominate in most schools (2005).

You have to give educators credit; for all the superficial comforts of being left alone, they will admit that constructive collaboration would lead to greatly improved instruction. As Dan Lortie found, even talented teachers know their limitations; most are "hesitant and uneasy" about the effectiveness of their teaching (1975, p. 210). When interviewing effective teachers, I'm impressed with how aware they are that isolation hides and protects ineffective practices and practitioners. And they privately lament the fact that their principals don't take a serious interest in what they teach or how well.

By elevating privacy and isolation in the name of professionalism, we have allowed teaching to acquire an outsized aura of mystique and complexity, a sense that effective teaching is primarily personal and therefore beyond scrutiny. This tendency was abetted by an excessive insistence that every child and every class of students is different. Therefore, we can't make generalizations about practice. As Elmore observes, teaching is increasingly regarded as an "an idiosyncratic and mysterious process that varies with each teacher" (2000, p. 16).

It has become increasingly difficult to ask practitioners to conform to even the most well-established elements of good instruction: being clear and explicit about what is to be learned and assessed; using assessments to evaluate a lesson's effectiveness and making constructive adjustments on the basis of results; conducting a check for understanding at certain points in a lesson; having kids read for higher-order purposes and write regularly; and clearly explicating and carefully teaching the criteria by which student work will be scored or evaluated.

Believe it or don't: these very basic practices are surprisingly rare, even in schools with respectable test scores. Isolation—"professional privacy" as Little called it—explains why "exemplary practices never take root in more than a small proportion of classrooms and schools" (Tyack & Cuban, as cited in Elmore, 2000, p. 6). Such lack of collaboration surely explains why "high-yield" strategies occur in only a tiny percentage of the 1,500 classrooms visited by researchers in the Learning 24/7 study (Learning 24/7, 2005).

Killing Teachers Softly: The Consequences of Isolation

Freedom isn't free. This soft, easy ethos of privacy, of the "inviolability of individual teachers' choices" has had catastrophic consequences for teachers and teaching. It ensures that principals are gun-shy about offering the most necessary correctives or advice for even the most blatantly poor practices. Rick DuFour's audiences laugh when he tells them that his teachers used to remind him to avoid ever using the word "should" in evaluations.

There are contradictions here. In the midst of this isolated, anything-goes culture, we continue to attend conferences and workshops and make frequent references to "the research." But as Goodlad and his colleagues told us long ago, isolation ensures that new learning seldom leads to changes in practice—in what teachers teach or how well they teach (1970, p. 72).

Even the National Staff Development Council has run a series of gutsy advertisements in *Phi Delta Kappan* and elsewhere asserting that most staff development is "irrelevant," "inadequate," "unfocused"—even "a complete waste of time" (*Phi Delta Kappan*, 2004). Moreover, my experience confirms the evidence that teachers mutely tolerate even the most inane and irrelevant presentations without ever rising up to reject this insulting infringement on their time (Chase, 1998).

We have struck a strange bargain: if you sit through our workshops, we promise not to make any real claims on your time or practice. We'll allow you to work alone while assuming (wrongly) that our programs and training are having a positive impact on practice, despite the lack of team-based efforts to implement and adjust practice on the basis of assessment results.

Isolation, both cause and consequence of the buffer, does have its compensations. As a teacher, I quickly realized that teaching was one of the safest and most secure of professions. There was even a certain cold comfort, for myself and my colleagues, in being left almost entirely alone. No one ever asked me or my English-teaching peers what we taught or if we followed a curriculum. No one ever asked how much reading students did (not much), or how much writing was taught (even less, I learned). No one would ever ask us to look at or—heaven forbid—adjust our instruction in light of assessment results (unimaginable).

We were kept from seeing evidence that some teachers were vastly more effective than others—that our most effective colleagues were having as much as six times the impact of those in the lowest third (Haycock & Huang, 2001).

Institutionalizing Mediocrity

Harvard's Tony Wagner writes of how enforced isolation ensures that "most of us in education are mediocre at what we do." From student teaching through tenure, he received no meaningful critique, no support, no feedback. He wryly concludes that

> I was proficient at everything, it seemed. . . . A unique experience? Hardly. Many veteran teachers chose the profession because they wanted security and autonomy, and so most schools and districts are organized to maintain this status quo. (2004, p. 40-41)

We have to take responsibility for the message this lack of feedback sends to teachers: that teaching, the soul of their chosen profession, doesn't much matter. Feel free to be an effective teacher, but it is not a requirement. Evaluations are occasional and meaningless (Marshall, 2005). Barring some grave, usually noninstructional malfeasance, you will never lose your job. One study showed that superintendents would have liked to remove about 1 in every 25 teachers, but only removed 1 in 600 (Gordon, 2005, p. 26). In Los Angeles Unified Schools, with its 35,000 teachers, the board tried to remove 400 incompetent teachers. The resistance was so fierce that the board succeeded in removing only one teacher during a two-year period. In the

New York City school system, with 72,000 teachers, only three were dismissed during a two-year period (Hess, 2004, p. 124). In the entire state of California, only 62 teachers out of 220,000 lost their jobs in one five-year period (Miller, 2003, p. 123). We are to suppose that the rest are teaching competently and effectively.

But teachers themselves, as Matt Miller found, know better. They recognize the marked differences in effectiveness among their colleagues. Good teachers told him that the "incompetence of their colleagues is appalling" (2003, p. 116). The former head of the American Federation of Teachers, Sandra Feldman, agreed, telling Miller that there are an alarming number of incompetent teachers being allowed to teach (2003, p. 123). Imagine the impact this is having on real kids, by the millions, whose names and faces are familiar to us. They don't have a chance until this situation changes. Until it does, teachers have no possibility of working in a profession where good performance can lead to higher levels of compensation.

I believe that the majority of "incompetent" teachers are potentially quite competent—if given the opportunity to work in a redefined system with colleagues and with cooperative supervision (discussed in Chapter 9). But teachers and students suffer terribly when we protect—when we buffer—teaching from inspection and scrutiny, and when we conveniently assume that "everyone is doing a good job." Like no other profession, we are denied the all-important opportunity to study and learn from our actions *and our results*. Hence, instructional decisions get "buried in the individual decisions of classroom teachers and buffered from external scrutiny" (Elmore, 2000, p. 9). Such ignorance is bliss. But it is hurting kids and teachers as it allows us ever so mistakenly "to assign causality to . . . weak family structures, poverty, discrimination, lack of aptitude, peer pressure, etc."

Such fatalism is a direct result of the buffer, the quiet but pervasive "superstructure" that is death to smart, constructive improvement efforts. And it is death to leadership, which is then diverted to the hugely wasteful business of protecting teaching "from outside inspection, interference, or disruption" (Elmore, 2000, p. 6).

3 Leadership Interrupted
How the Buffer Compromises Supervision

We can create the most effective generation of leaders ever by redefining and simplifying leadership around the core concepts of professional learning communities. But no one can lead in an environment where differences in practice and learning outcomes are ignored or trivialized. No one can lead effectively where constructive feedback is regarded as an invasion of privacy, an affront to professionalism.

This is mostly our fault, not the fault of teachers. Over time, we created what Kim Marshall calls "an emptiness in the professional relationship between teachers and school leaders" (2005, p. 730). The institutional muscles—the willingness to monitor, critique, and confront when necessary—which are so vital to improvement in every other profession, have atrophied. Leaders long ago made their peace with this arrangement (Evans, 1996; Elmore, 2000).

This relationship perpetuates a disheartening but "consistent pattern: direct involvement in instruction is among the least frequent activities performed by administrators of any kind at any level" (Elmore, 2000, p. 6).

The Leadership Illusion

It's this simple: schools won't improve until the average building leader begins to work cooperatively with teachers to truly, meaningfully oversee and improve instructional quality. These arrangements can begin in any individual school and under any reasonably intelligent leader, as we'll see in Chapter 9. But it will be difficult to enter what Marzano calls an "era of unprecedented effectiveness" (2003) without strong, focused support from districts and state departments, as we'll see in Chapter 10.

In the meantime, our typical attempts to reform our schools will not only fail but will have a corrupting effect as we engage in the pretense of instructional improvement. Elmore tells us that most administrative preparation programs talk a lot about instructional leadership. We give lip service to the "central position of instruction" in administration. But all this apparent emphasis on instruction, he notes,

> is mainly just talk. In fact, few administrators of any kind or at any level are directly involved in instruction. Principals who develop skills and knowledge required to become instructional leaders do so because of their own preferences and values—and often at some cost to their own careers. (1999-2000, p. 9)

We need to own up to the fact that school leaders usually have little effect on instruction. Even teachers admit this (Elmore, 2000, p. 17). Robert Evans has noted that most administrators learn quickly to accommodate themselves to the status quo, and that they are

> untrained for leading [instructional] change. They have been socialized to be maintainers. . . . Almost everything one learns as a principal reinforces the old congressional saw: to get along, go along." (1996, p. 203)

When administrators "go along" instead of leading, they perpetuate mediocrity. Subtle institutional forces urge them to accommodate or wink at inferior practice, while implying to their communities that instruction is effective or "good enough." We can only imagine the psychic toll this takes on many of them.

But there is a logic here: it is imperative for professionals entrusted with people's children to inspire confidence in parents and communities, to project an image of quality. The buffer has been enormously effective here: despite the brutal facts already enumerated, parents tend to think highly of their local schools.

Some of the most conscientious, well-educated parents have a hard time believing that the apparatus of leadership and supervision—teacher evaluation, improvement planning, and staff development—has almost no impact on what teachers do in their classrooms (Schmoker, 2004; Marshall, 2005; Corcoran, Fuhrman, & Belcher, 2001).

This "logic of confidence," as Elmore calls it (2000, p. 7), is quite different from the logic of quality, which would force a constructive encounter with both good and poor teaching. The logic of confidence makes no such demands.

The Logic of Confidence

An enormous amount of precious time is diverted from authentic leadership and instructional improvement to maintaining this logic of confidence. We invest time and money in high-sounding plans and new programs we roll out each year with great fanfare. Because people conflate "change" with improvement, schools are

> almost always aboil with some kind of "change" but they are only rarely involved in any deliberate process of *improvement,* where progress is checked against a clearly specified instructional goal. (Elmore, 2000, p. 7)

Logically—sadly—administrators tend to be "hired and retained on the basis of their capacity to buffer teachers from outside interference...to support the prevailing logic of confidence," Elmore notes (2000, p. 7).

One of the most insidious forms of this logic can be seen in schools' aggressive efforts to win state or regional awards. When the awards roll in, banners are hung, and newspapers publicize these honors. Enrollment goes up, as parents begin to move into the attendance area of these award-winning schools. The administrators who led the charge are often promoted. School boards and district offices like nothing better than to point with pride at the "A+" schools in their midst. Everyone's happy.

But few ask the basic question: on what basis do schools earn these coveted awards? The reasons may surprise us.

Rewarding Mediocrity

Ironies abound here. Applying for these awards consumes precious time that could be spent on allowing teachers to collaboratively improve lessons and assessments—which would have a direct and immediate impact on student learning.

With notable occasional exceptions, these awards are usually given *irrespective of instructional quality or gains in achievement* (this is beginning to change under the No Child Left Behind law). Historically, those who make these selections know almost nothing about the two things that matter most: what is being taught and how well. The school visits they conduct are shallow, cursory affairs.

These awards are usually earned on the basis of how many committee meetings our staffs are willing to endure; how many forms we can fill out; how many unproven, attractively titled or brand-name programs we are willing to launch and describe in florid detail—a tremendous distraction from authentic instructional improvement efforts.

Such programs make the hard, ongoing work of improving lessons and assessments seem pedestrian. Launching a series of workshops or a grant-funded program or a "(fill in the blank) academy" sounds great but seldom affects the quality of instruction. We now know that these programs and training sessions themselves are rarely selected on the basis of evidence or proven effectiveness (Corcoran, Fuhrman, & Belcher, 2001). Once launched, we don't monitor to ensure that they result in more coherent curriculum or effective teaching. This isn't how the game is played.

Maybe worst of all, these awards inspire baseless confidence in the status quo—not only among the public but among educators themselves, who become doubly complacent about correcting the shortcomings already described. Why should they? They are an "A+" school. I worked in one of these schools; even the principal knew it was a charade but felt pressured to pursue it. My own kids have attended award-winning schools where the principals had no idea what teachers were teaching. By any objective standard, literacy instruction was a shambles, and teachers readily admitted that they didn't teach writing.

Ironically, I know of several cases where staff members spent years of their time and energy helping a school or administrator win the most prestigious state and national awards. But genuine instructional improvement occurred only and immediately *after the departure of the award-winning administrator.*

Perhaps nothing reflects the logic of confidence better than the aura of prestige that surrounds the U.S. Department of Education Blue Ribbon award. Years ago, a group of us called a handful of these award winners to find out how they had (presumably) raised achievement. To our surprise, none had. Although these schools had launched lots of programs, we found not a single case of exceptional achievement or improvement. Even the Department of Education finally owned up to the fact that most schools received the award for reasons other than excellence in teaching and achievement (Loveless & DiPerna, 2000). Finally, in 2002 the department began using academic superiority and dramatic gains in student achievement in their criteria for these awards. For years, very few schools earned these awards for legitimate achievements.

Sometimes entire districts have played this game. My daughters attended an award-winning school in an award-winning district. At both the district and school levels, administrators made polished presentations about the importance of standards. Every parent was given an expensive, multifold, grade-by-grade list of what children would be taught. We were emphatically assured that our children would learn these standards, that the schools were organized to teach them.

But a group of us (including some educational researchers) made an interesting discovery: that there wasn't the slightest resemblance between those lists and what our children were taught. Teachers were quite candid about this; several informed me that their principal never so much as asked if they taught to these standards.

An even more common form of the buffer and the logic of confidence can be seen in our annual or multiyear "strategic" or "school improvement plans." Like awards, these are represented to our communities as though they are meaningful and effective.

The Mirage of School Improvement Planning

Certainly, by now, schools should know that "strategic planning doesn't work"—and never did (Kouzes & Posner, 1995, p. 244). Like so many initiatives, it was embraced on a massive scale in the absence of any evidence of effectiveness. As Bruce Joyce writes, elaborate improvement planning "has failed miserably and in plain sight" (2004, p. 76).

But damn the facts. Schools, districts, and state education departments continue to commit to these multipage planning templates that guarantee "fragmentation and overload" (Fullan, 1996, p. 420)—and thus failure. A recent study in Kentucky confirmed what was already abundantly clear: that the most common, elaborate forms of improvement planning have a *negative* relationship to achievement (Kannapel & Clements, 2005); they reduce the chances for improvement. "Formal planning," Pfeffer and Sutton write, is "essentially unrelated to organizational performance" (2000, p. 43). The best studies point to how this model diverts organizations from their core purposes. Collins observes that such plans ensure that organizations become "scattered and diffused, moving on many levels"—doomed to "pursue many ends at the same time" (2001a, p. 91; for a full treatment of this issue, see Schmoker, 2004).

It turns out that "simple plans" work best—those with a direct focus on straightforward actions and opportunities (Collins, 2001a, p. 177). In education, we need to stay focused on the opportunities we've already described. To address these clear shortcomings, our best "plan" is to arrange for teachers to analyze their achievement data, set goals, and then meet at least twice a month—for 45 minutes or so. That way, they can help one another ensure that they are teaching essential standards and using assessment results to improve the quality of their lessons.

I've looked at hundreds of plans, almost all done in accordance with templates required by well-meaning districts, accreditation agencies, and state education departments. I've gone over these templates with officials from these agencies. Even they admit, on close examination, to the havoc that is wrought by these lengthy, ambiguously worded documents.

Then why do we persist? One state education department document contained more than 130 requirements. A state official agreed with me that any five of these could overwhelm most schools or systems while having little or no impact on what is taught or how well. We agreed that these templates precluded focused effort. But the official said what I often hear: that too many people had invested too much time in these plans and processes and they couldn't be changed.

Yes, they can. And they must. We'll explore this thoroughly in Chapters 9 and 10. In one district where I worked, we couldn't resist the allure of elaborate "school improvement planning," despite the absence of evidence that it had been effective anywhere. We were convinced that the needs assessments and surveys and programs and workshops and conference attendance and staff development days and book studies and action steps that filled the columns and boxes of our thick plans would have a palpable effect on instruction. We were wrong; like most staff development efforts, ours looked great but were wired for failure (Guskey, 2003; Stiggins, 1999; Corcoran, Fuhrman, & Belcher, 2001; Schmoker, 2004).

All this planning and training ensured "lots of change, but not much improvement" (Elmore, 2000, p. 12). It diverted us from focusing on the most starkly simple elements of quality and improvement—like a common curriculum, the lack of which made improvement impossible. Curricular chaos may be the most destructive, if unintended, effect of the buffer. In the next chapter, we'll see how teachers can work together to bring order to that chaos—an order that focuses on student achievement.

4 | **Curricular Chaos**

If you care about schools, the curricular chaos within them has to arrest your attention. Remember the premise: the uglier the problem, the bigger the educational payoff in solving the problem. There's one hell of a payoff here.

Curriculum: A Very Big Deal

I want to be as emphatic as possible: the impact of the actual, taught curriculum on school quality, on student learning, is indescribably important. Robert Marzano did a meta-analysis of in-school factors that affect student achievement. Coming in at the top—first place—is *what gets taught,* what he calls a "guaranteed and viable curriculum." That is, if teachers can lay out a sound—a viable—set of standards and can then guarantee (more or less) that these standards actually get taught, we can raise levels of achievement immensely.

There's nothing complex here. For decades, Larry Lezotte has been telling audiences that children can learn only what we teach them but that "there is a huge gap between what is taught and what is tested" (as cited in Sparks, 2001b, p. 33). Andrew Porter, a researcher at Vanderbilt University, writes that "What gets taught is the strongest single predictor of gains in achievement." But he then adds, somewhat ominously, that "regardless of what a state policy or a district curriculum spells out, the classroom teacher decides . . . what topics to cover" (Manzo, 2003b, p. 8).

And there's the rub. In any school or district, you'll find copies of "curriculum guides" kicking around. But does anyone follow them? Heidi Hayes Jacobs likes to ask her audiences "What is a curriculum guide?" Her answer: "a well-intended fiction."

I once examined a thick curriculum guide—years in the making—with an assistant superintendent of instruction in a Midwestern district. When I asked her how much influence this document had on what was actually taught, she paused and then said, "None." We had to laugh.

The buffer keeps all of us—communities, administrators, and teachers—from coming to terms with this stark reality of schools, despite the illimitable damage it has inflicted on children and learning. Curricular chaos continues to be among the best-kept secrets in education. As Marzano points out, the "discrepancy between the intended curriculum and the implemented curriculum comes as a surprise to noneducators and educators alike" (2003, p. 23). On this incalculably important factor, with the learning of millions of children hanging in the balance, we operate in the dim half-light of denial.

Overwhelming Evidence of Inconsistency

The evidence for this discrepancy is conclusive. David Berliner's team of researchers found that within the same school and grade level, chaos reigns. One teacher taught 28 times as much science as a teacher down the hall, and no one in the school knew this until the researchers went in (1984, p. 53).

Similarly, a research group investigated which standards were actually taught in hundreds of schools and compared the list against the state-assessed standards. There was almost no correspondence. They found redundancy and inconsistency at every grade level; what did get taught was taught *down*. By 5th grade, most students were being given 2nd and 3rd grade material. Teacher comments were telling: "Are we teaching below grade level?" one asked. "I have been teaching what I always did," said another (DataWorks Assessment Newsletter, 2000, p. 2). Doug Reeves, who seldom minces words, observes that

> You can walk into any school system, large or small, and ask to see samples of work that's proficient from five different 4th-grade classrooms. You'll get five radically different qualities of work. (as cited in Sausner, 2005, p. 32)

Finally: a recent study in 11 states and 5 urban districts found that "instruction is not adequately aligned with state assessments and standards." The study cites a frustrated assistant superintendent who remarked, "When teachers see what they are doing, it is often not what they think they are doing" (Manzo, 2003b, p. 1). In the buffered, hands-off management culture of the average school, teaching devolves into what Susan Rosenholtz calls "a self-selected jumble" of standards, of isolated teachers' preferences—with no connection to any common curriculum (1991). If this approach guarantees anything, it is "curricular chaos," fragmentation, and failure (Schmoker & Marzano, 1999). This is the result of decades of benign neglect, of failing—out of a misguided respect for autonomy and "professionalism"—to monitor which standards are actually taught.

You can't "guarantee" what you don't monitor. Every audience of teachers I have ever spoken with agrees that testing and accountability are still having only a marginal and uneven effect on the actual, taught curriculum in English, reading, and language arts (as we'll see in Chapter 7). In math, they agree that *the math textbook* is still the de facto curriculum—but that teachers make entirely idiosyncratic use of these textbooks. Marzano cites the case of a teacher who is asked why she doesn't teach fractions. Her reply: I don't like fractions. Marzano concludes that "the notion of a coherent implemented curriculum . . . is a myth" (2003, p. 23).

The Good News

If ever a grave problem pointed to an equally rich opportunity, this is it. At Roosevelt Middle School, near Detroit, science scores were, as principal William Hardy put it, "in the tank." They found that "curriculum didn't match" the assessed standards, so they organized standards into three 12-week units to create a "more focused curriculum." The result: 92 percent of 8th graders scored at the top two levels, compared with 66 percent of students statewide (Higgins, 2002, pp. 1–2). In nearby Southfield, Michigan, Principal Anthony Muhammad ensured that teams of teachers carefully scheduled when they would teach the most essential state standards and that the teams monitored their progress. Over a three-year period, scores in every category went up by an average of 24 points (A. Muhammad, personal communication, May 2005).

A caveat: when it comes to curriculum and standards, teachers need and deserve some flexibility; we need to allow for personal and creative variation—some serendipity— and the right to simply reject a standard on plausible grounds.

But not chaos. We'll look at ways to monitor curriculum—what's actually taught—in Chapter 9, which deals with leadership in the learning community. For now, let's look at a set of particularly simple, powerful tools for promoting a "guaranteed and viable curriculum."

Overlooked Opportunity: Sample Tests and State Assessment Guides

If we truly grasp the importance of a "guaranteed and viable curriculum" then it is time we took advantage of the tools available to us for ensuring it. Almost every state provides an array of materials that would help teachers align their curriculum with state assessments.

What do we find in many of these free materials? Entire sample tests for every subject and grade level. In math, the sample tests and items are accompanied not only by an answer key but by detailed explanations for how problems could be solved.

In most states, booklets are provided that contain illustrative examples of student written work, from poor to excellent. They are scored, for each criterion, using the state rubric. Furthermore, the scores are accompanied by invaluable explanations with respect to each element of the rubric.

In reading, many states provide sample passages and questions, along with written responses for the predominantly *higher-order* reading standards contained in most state exams (the ones we should focus on). The prevalence of higher-order standards surprises many educators but is borne out by a recent review of state assessments that found that almost all of the items on these tests—an encouraging trend—are higher-order and inferential in nature (Liben & Liben, 2005). I support James Popham and others who are calling for new—more expensive—state exams that assess the most essential higher-order reading standards in the most meaningful fashion (Popham, 2004). But in the meantime, it is heartening that state reading assessments are increasingly dominated by skills such as the ability to infer; to identify an author's bias or persuasive techniques; to support interpretations or main ideas with evidence from the text; and to summarize, synthesize, analyze, and evaluate.

Keep in mind that no state could possibly assess every state standard in its exhaustive "state standards" lists or documents (Schmoker & Marzano, 1999). We wouldn't want them to. That's why these sample tests and assessment guides are invaluable. Most urge a necessary economy, a focus on those standards that the state deems most important. They allow teachers to focus on fewer standards, and that approach is essential to effective teaching and learning.

Worried about narrowing the curriculum? Don't be. In international comparisons, the highest-scoring countries attempt to teach *less than a third* as many topics as those found in U.S. textbooks. "Narrowing the curriculum," when done right, is not just permissible but essential. The need to tighten the focus may explain why fully two-thirds of high school teachers in Massachusetts did not see such narrowing (per their state assessments) as having any negative impact on teaching and learning (Kurtz, 2003).

By focusing on important standards and using tools such as sample tests, teachers can help their students understand what they need to learn—and what they will be tested on. To a great degree, these materials give the game away. And they help us to see that state assessments, however imperfect, are not the enemy. As Grant Wiggins writes, "the problem is not with tests per se, but the failure . . . to be results-focused and data-driven" (1994, p. 18). I have found that the more closely teachers study these materials, the less critical they are of standards and testing—and the more apt they are to see that the tests actually guide them toward essential skills in math, reading, and writing. Wiggins and McTighe cite numerous studies that conclude that "authentic pedagogy . . . higher-order thinking and deep-knowledge approaches" have significantly more impact on student performance than low-level pedagogy (2005, pp. 306–307).

The bottom line is that if we taught math, writing, and critical reading effectively, exactly as we know they should be taught, then students would do exceedingly well on state assessments. On a cautionary note, I'm not as sure of this approach in science and social studies. I believe we need to move more slowly and carefully in these subjects, where the temptation is to test too many facts at the expense of critical understanding.

Now, one might assume that these materials would be eagerly sought and studied by teachers. They're not—although this too may be starting to change. Many don't even know these documents exist or where to find them. This lack of awareness allows teachers to indulge in a misinformed rejection of testing, in clichés about their reputedly "lower-order" emphases, and in other myths. Tests aren't perfect; the better news is that the best kind of teaching guarantees success on these assessments (Wiggins, 1998, p. 320).

In all the hustle and fanfare of planning, of rolling out new programs, of working to meet accreditation requirements, here is another example of our failure to take full advantage of an invaluable resource that would have a direct impact on achieving a guaranteed and viable curriculum—arguably the single most important pre-condition for improvement. All we have to do is to give these documents to teachers, explain their contents, and ensure their frequent use.

How are real schools and students affected by our failure to systematically monitor and improve curriculum and instruction, by our failure to take advantage of even the simplest mechanisms, materials, and opportunities for improvement? If we enlarge the concept of "curriculum" to include the totality of instruction, of what is taught and how well, a sobering picture emerges—and a wonderful opportunity.

The Buffer: Real Schools, Real Consequences

An elementary school in a large urban area is only too typical. "Strip away the love and hard work," and you find a school where performance is still abysmal (Kossan, 2004, p. B1). It is staffed—take note— with experienced teachers. Funds have allowed the school to reduce class size and to offer both preschool and kindergarten.

But there's no improvement. A close look by state "solutions teams" revealed the real problems—none of them a matter of the usual excuses. The teams

> found what many other solutions teams have found at other under-performing schools in the state: a culture where teachers did their own thing . . . and lesson plans that weren't based on [state] learning goals. (Kossan, 2004, p. B2)

Sometimes the truth, if only for a moment, slips through the buffer. The district where this school is located recently hired a new superintendent. Upon arriving, he boldly announced that he had found the district to be "a ship adrift." He found "no consistent curriculum" in any of the schools. Teachers worked in isolation and never talked to each other. Teachers had no idea what their same-grade counterparts were teaching next door. Even so, teachers routinely told principals "I do this. I know it works. Who are you to tell me different?" The new superintendent "heard the same excuse at every school: 'You don't understand our kids.'"

His conclusion about such curricular chaos and excuses? "It's criminal" (Kossan, 2004, p. B2).

Wish him well. The parents and students in his community don't know how lucky they are. Because such straight talk—the beginning of improvement—is rare in superintendents.

As we've seen, most schools are similarly adrift when it comes to make-or-break factors such as a guaranteed and viable curriculum. For all the damage this lack of consistency brings, it is still under the radar: you won't read about "curricular chaos" on the education page of the local newspaper; you won't hear a serious discussion about the general mediocrity of lessons and assessments at a school board meeting.

Here's another revealing case of the buffer at work, right down the road from Richard Elmore's office at Harvard. In a candid account, researcher Pedro Noguera describes 10 schools in Boston Public that "had experimented with a variety of reform strategies" (2004, p. 26). But a close look revealed the same pattern; the research team discovered that the reform effort was "disorganized, poorly managed" (p. 28). In one class, the team observed how a long-term substitute was routinely taking attendance and then reading the newspaper. The principal said she was aware of the situation—then did nothing about it. In another class, *even as the study was being conducted,* most students were being allowed to play cards—every day.

Throughout the study, the team "saw a tremendous gap between the intent of the reforms and their implementation." At most of the schools, the reforms "had not changed the quality of instruction that students received" (Noguera, p. 29). Many teachers hadn't even heard of the reforms. Nor had students, who reported that they hadn't noticed any changes in the school as a result of the reforms. At 8 of these 10 schools, there were no achievement gains.

The Importance of Quality Control

Throughout this hard-hitting piece, Noguera describes such abuses as the result of a pervasive, dismaying lack of "quality control" in schools, without which "we have little reason to believe that schools will improve" (p. 30). Savor the researchers' profound, if understated conclusion: "Improvements in teaching and learning can only come from a strategy *focused on improving instruction*" (Noguera, 2004, p. 30) (emphasis added).

Now take a high-performing college preparatory school, with mostly smart, socially advantaged students. But as in most schools, there was, until recently, very limited oversight of curriculum or instruction. Because of this, no one knew if or to what extent essential standards were being taught. An inordinate amount of class time was spent completing worksheets. Students were rarely asked to closely read texts for analytical or evaluative purposes. They wrote even less. Writing was largely confined to book reports, even as some teachers allowed students to make a poster or mobile as a substitute for writing (as though such projects have ever helped students to write effectively or to acquire a deeper understanding of a text). Students didn't use and were not taught to understand the state writing rubric. Several teachers expressed the belief that rubrics and scoring guides "stifled creativity." On those few occasions when students wrote, it was in one draft, during a single class period, with no clear criteria for how their writing would be evaluated. Papers were usually returned several weeks after they were completed, without any written feedback and with no opportunity for students to revise their writing or even reflect on the quality of their written work.

All of these realities were hidden behind their high scores. Imagine the staggering amount of academic and intellectual potential that was being wasted.

This is the logical conclusion of allowing the buffer, the "inviolability of the classroom" to prevent us from seeing how much better instruction could be, in almost every school.

A study of 28 urban districts found that these problems are common, that we have yet to institute even the most basic elements of quality control—such as monitoring curriculum—in schools where they are so desperately needed (Petrides & Nodine, 2005).

There are exceptions—teachers, schools, and districts that break the mold. But in the main, wherever I have toured classrooms, always with other educators, we have found this same predominant inattention to what is taught and how well. Again and again, we see incoherent curricula, ineffective instruction and assessment practices, and no quality control. We continue to find programs, workshops, and improvement plans that don't acknowledge or address the need for better instruction and its supervision.

The Way Out

Now let's examine a success story, also from Boston, that captures the promise of all that we have been discussing here. Kim Marshall, a former principal, writes in the *Kappan* (2003) about the journey taken by his poor, high-minority elementary school. For years, he struggled heroically against the curriculum anarchy, low expectations, and arbitrary grading practices that prevailed in his school and ensured student failure for decades. It was a tough time for Marshall; educators know how painful it can be to go it alone against a resistant faculty.

Marshall was more persistent and courageous than any principal should have to be—for merely asking his faculty for only the most sensible, reasonable improvements to instruction and curriculum. But the resisters won out.

Until, that is, accountability arrived in earnest in Massachusetts. When Mather Elementary received an "underperforming" label, faculty members were embarrassed—and more receptive to change. Marshall had his teachers, in teams, examine the assessed standards. They found what so many teachers discover when they examine these documents carefully: that the tests "really did measure the kinds of skills and knowledge students needed to be successful" (Marshall, 2003, p. 112). They then began to align their curriculum to the state assessment, and to work in teams to help one another develop lessons that would ensure higher rates of student success.

With these elements in place, Mather made appreciable improvements and "with amazing speed." Levels of learning, previously rock bottom in citywide standings, rose to the top third. Mather made the greatest gains of any large elementary school in the state of Massachusetts.

Not one of these factors—exceptional leadership, teaming, clear standards, or accountability—by itself made the difference at Mather. But *in combination,* these factors guarantee that any school will make rapid, substantial improvements. Nationwide, standards are becoming clearer and schools are more accountable than ever. And as this book goes to press, some positive achievement trends are being reported at the elementary level. But pervasive, large-scale improvement won't occur until we create conditions where average principals aren't forced to overcome fierce resistance to the most reasonable requirements: a coherent, high-quality curriculum, reasonably well-taught.

Like the medical community after 1910, education must own up, collectively, to the gap between what we know and what we do, between "what we've always done" and what our clients need. Public schools, as an institution, must care enough about kids to be unafraid to express, in Roland Barth's words, our "moral outrage at ineffective practices" (2002, p. 10).

In the education professions, including higher education, an honest encounter with the brutal facts will unleash untold amounts of talent from students, teachers, and administrators. We must make preparations for this encounter.

The Truth Will Set Us Free

We might liken this encounter to another harsh and admittedly imperfect analogy.

Before World War II, there was relatively little travel between the North and Deep South. This lack of interaction helped perpetuate the complacent acceptance of Jim Crow racism. Polls indicated that most Americans did not think that blacks were unfairly treated (Barone, 2004, pp. 48–50).

Most Americans, had they encountered these conditions, would have found them abhorrent. But the South—like today's classrooms—was isolated, insular. Migration in the United States was to the north, not the south. Even brief, disturbing sojourns by Northerners weren't enough to quicken action—to break through the buffer of half-truths and cultural isolation. Life went on, justified by long-accepted clichés about the complexity and inevitability of it all.

Then, quite suddenly, everything changed. There were many factors at work, but two especially powerful forces converged: the media and Martin Luther King Jr. King saw that vivid, unremitting doses of unpleasant truth would shake people from their complacency. In 1963, he and his organizers persuaded hundreds of students and schoolchildren to begin sitting at segregated lunch counters, to begin using segregated restrooms and drinking fountains. The predictable reaction: demonstrators were attacked with fire hoses and police dogs. At a time when news coverage was being extended and expanded, all this made national news, despite local efforts to buffer—to suppress—these realities. Audiences recoiled, and the wheels of change began to turn (Halberstam, 1993, pp. 82–92; Barone, 2004, pp. 49–50).

A tipping point had been reached. Polling data did a reversal; it now reflected America's encounter with the brutal facts. Action followed awareness, as an honest reckoning with these facts led to historic changes.

But the civil rights agenda is not complete. Education is at the heart of what remains to be accomplished (Ackerman, 2004; Ferguson & Mehta, 2004, p. 658). The key to education may very well be literacy—which, I'll argue, we don't yet adequately understand. The need and opportunity for improvement in this area cannot be overstated. In the next section, we'll see how a new conception of literacy and literacy instruction will promote thought and learning in every discipline, and will have the most prodigious and immediate impact on our ability to truly provide "equal citizenship for all" (Gordon 2005, p. 26).

Section II

Literacy Education:
The Greatest Opportunity of All

Underdeveloped literacy skills are the number one reason why students are retained, assigned to special education, given long-term remedial services, and why they fail to graduate from high school.

—Vincent Ferrandino and Gerald Tirozzi

We've seen how the buffer pervades our school system, how it impedes us in our efforts to monitor and improve the content and quality of instruction. I would argue that it has had an especially frightful impact in the area of literacy instruction. This focus is not in any way intended to diminish the importance of other disciplines. The purpose of these next three chapters is to reveal, by focusing on one crucial area, the scale of the opportunity we have for better schools.

In Chapter 5, we will take a general look at the social, intellectual, and economic power of acquiring the most authentic forms of literacy—of purposeful, intellectually engaging reading, writing, and discussion.

In Chapter 6, we will examine the powerful (if seldom heard) case for each of these three components of authentic literacy. A new understanding of literacy is essential to the deep changes we must make to literacy instruction, which, as we'll see, would transform and enliven learning for both students and teachers—in every subject area.

In Chapter 7, I'll describe, in detail, what could be education's most consummate opportunity: the conspicuous gap between this powerful (but hardly exotic) conception of literacy and its real-world counterpart: the startling actualities of literacy instruction in most classrooms.

In Appendix A, we'll look at some practical, adaptable ways we could implement this new model of literacy instruction in virtually any course. Such a change would transform average schools into intellectually vibrant places that prepare students for college, for life, and the life of the mind.

5 | The Power of *Authentic* Literacy

Adolescents entering the adult world in the 21st century will read and write more than at any other time in human history. They will need advanced levels of literacy to perform their jobs, run their households, act as citizens, and conduct their personal lives.

—Richard Vacca

Imagine . . . *all students, regardless of socioeconomic circumstance, having spent most of their class time in English, social studies, and other courses closely and carefully reading, rereading, discussing, and writing about the ideas in various texts. Imagine every student graduating from high school having analyzed and imitated excellent examples of adult writing and having written countless close literary analyses, essays, grant proposals, business plans, and position papers on multiple political, scientific, and cultural controversies—after carefully reading and discussing two or more conflicting documents on innumerable engaging issues.*

As ambitious as this vision may sound, we have more than enough time—12 years!—to provide an ample amount of such experiences, which would shatter achievement records, reduce dropouts, and ensure college readiness and graduation rates at levels never achieved. Many students would graduate from high school educated as well as or better than many current college graduates. If such experiences were common—and they could be—our schools would be second to none.

The lifelong consequences of good—or poor—literacy skills are monumental. Whether we acquire them in science, social studies, or English, they affect not only school success, but intelligence itself—our ability to think. Authentic literacy, rightly acquired, profoundly affects students' life and career options, their understanding of the world, their facility with concepts and ideas. These intellectual abilities pervade every subject area. For these reasons, we need to have the deepest and most complete understanding of what literacy is and how students can best acquire it. Effective literacy strategies are far simpler than much that we've been told.

The Way Up and Out

In his classic book, *Lives on the Boundary,* Mike Rose describes his school experience growing up poor in east Los Angeles. In his family's tiny house, he shared a bedroom with his parents. Rose attended school in a state of "somnambulism"—of sleepy, bored frustration. For him and many of his classmates, school was a place of "embarrassment, not challenge" (1989, p. 31). He saw his own probable future in the "ravaged hope," the lack of curiosity and passion so sadly characteristic of the adults he grew up around (p. 47).

Until, that is, he entered the 10th grade. That's when Jack MacFarland became his English teacher. MacFarland—without the benefit of "standards"—taught to the very best standards we find in state assessments. He did this by teaching English in a way that is entirely at odds with conventional literacy instruction.

Rose and his classmates began to read a multitude of books, articles, and essays—*in class*—and to talk and write about the issues raised in their reading. MacFarland was constantly asking prepared questions as his students "wrote and talked, wrote and talked" about what they read, closely and purposefully, every day (Rose, pp. 32–34). This simple formula—reading, writing, and talking—was the heart of their English instruction. It is the heart of authentic literacy.

Years later, Rose realized that MacFarland had provided a "prep school curriculum" for him and his fellow members of (savor the irony) the "Voc. Ed. Crowd" (pp. 32–33). In a single life-transforming year, Rose received the kind of authentic literacy education that he could have been getting for 12 years. It allowed him, against all expectations, to become the first member of his family to attend college. He is now a professor at UCLA.

Generous amounts of close, purposeful reading, rereading, writing, and talking, as underemphasized as they are in K–12 education, are the essence of authentic literacy. These simple activities are the foundation for a trained, powerful mind—and a promising future. They are the way up and out—of boredom, poverty, and intellectual inadequacy. And they're the ticket to ensuring that record numbers of minority and disadvantaged youngsters attend and graduate from college. We have yet to realize how much is at stake here.

Literacy, Liberation, and Opportunity

Rose grew up with a vivid sense of limits about his academic capabilities, which professions he could pursue, and which circles he could move in. But close reading, talking, and writing, in redundant abundance, changed all that. They rid him of his "sense of exclusion." Rose observes, "Jack MacFarland had saved me . . . and revitalized my mind." For the first time, Rose "felt freed, as if I were untying fetters" (pp. 46–47). This breakthrough paved the way for his future success. But as we'll see in the next chapter, prevailing language arts instruction actually *prevents* the poor—and poorly educated—from ever making this transition.

Rose, now literate, learned to *think*—to accurately and effectively weigh words and articulate ideas with skill and clarity. In this sense, the majority of students are indeed "on the boundary." Some are caught between a dismal and barely adequate education. Others are on the boundary between a mediocre education and one that more richly equips them for the intellectual demands and opportunities of the university, of professional and intellectual life.

When I taught English at a state university, I saw plenty of students on the boundary at the higher end. Although they were able to get into college, most of them wrote poorly. Critical and analytical reading and discussion, though engaging, was new for them. Almost half would never graduate, even with remedial help.

Wherever students are on this continuum, their intellectual and professional prospects can pivot hugely on how much reading, writing, and talking they do during their K–12 years.

Higher-Order Literacy Demands

Literacy expert Richard Allington, president of the International Reading Association for 2005–2006, has commented forcefully about this clear connection between authentic reading and writing experiences and students' personal, intellectual, and professional prospects. The "information age," he writes

> places higher-order literacy demands on all of us . . . these demands include synthesizing and evaluating information from multiple sources. American schools need to enhance the ability of children to search and sort through information, to synthesize and analyze the information they encounter. (2001, p. 7)

But, alas, Allington's research, like other studies we'll cite in the next chapter, reveals something deeply troubling: such intellectually substantive reading, writing, and talking are exceedingly rare in most classrooms. We should be alarmed by this fact. As Ferrandino and Tirozzi point out, literacy determines who will—or won't

> garner respect from peers and authority . . . it speaks to the larger societal issues of access and equity. In our society, being literate opens doors—and opens them wide. (2004, p. 29)

This kind of literacy goes way beyond "decoding" or "fluency," which are only the beginning of literacy. Test scores themselves show that most students who can read and decode are systematically denied the opportunity to acquire the kind of higher-order literacy that can make such a difference in our lives. The majority of every audience of teachers I've spoken to has acknowledged that we have a serious problem here.

Deborah Meier, the legendary inner-city principal, knows real literacy from its inferior substitutes. Her charter schools in New York and Boston have sent high proportions of disadvantaged and minority students to the best colleges. Very high proportions of these students graduate (Meier, 2002). She explicitly advocates the kind of literacy we'll describe here, which has enabled a remarkable number of students to break the bonds of class and race and become "powerful members of the ruling class." Such intellectual empowerment, she tells us emphatically, should be the "non-negotiable, central goal of public schooling" (Matthews, 2004, p. 3). For Meier,

> The question is not, Is it possible to educate all children well? But rather Do we want to do it badly enough? . . . There's a radical—and wonderful—new idea here: the idea that every citizen is capable of the kind of intellectual competence previously attained by only a small minority. . . . Children should be inventors of their own theories, critics of other peoples' ideas, analyzers of evidence, and makers of their own personal marks on this most complex world. (2002, p. 4)

Such a rigorous, intellectually robust education is eminently within the reach of our students (as I hope the questions and activities in Appendix A will help to make clear).

Habits of Mind

For Meier, intellectual, social, and economic power, the kind we desire for our own children, comes from activities any student can engage in tomorrow morning: large, daily doses of what Meier calls "deep reading," writing, and argument (more on this in a moment). In combination, these activities can animate students' interest in the ideas and people they encounter in texts—in other words, the characters and historical figures whose actions and remarks they can evaluate, condemn, or defend. Every day of their school lives, students should be reading texts critically, then weighing evidence for or against people, ideas, and policies, and forming opinions. These activities foster a set of essential, intellectual "habits of mind," as Meier and author Ted Sizer call them. These practices include the ability to

- Critically examine evidence in a text.

- See the world from multiple viewpoints.

- Make connections and detect patterns among ideas and perspectives.

- Imagine alternatives. (What if? What else?)

- Understand relevance: (What difference does it make?)

"What difference does it make?" is a question we often neglect to consider, which may account for why English is usually students' least favorite course.

This last point is important. If we took this analysis seriously, it would prevent a host of inane practices—endless time spent learning arcane literary terms, overanalyzing metaphors, and identifying elements such as "climax," "plot," or "rising action" (as though anyone ever reads that way). We should be focusing on how students feel about characters, on their thoughts and informed opinions about the themes and controversies in literature and nonfiction—as they write and talk about them.

Institutionally, we do not yet realize that 12 years of generous, daily amounts of *in-school* reading, writing, and discussion, built around good questions (shared and refined by teams and networks of teachers), would create unimagined intellectual, academic, and professional possibilities for our children.

This framework belongs in every subject and discipline. Certainly history and social studies provide some of the best opportunities for such text-based inquiry. Neil Postman suggests that English—language arts—is an especially natural place to foster these invaluable habits and capacities (Postman & Weingartner, 1969, p. 54).

It is through reading, writing, and talking that students most directly and effectively acquire a facility with what Lisa Delpit calls the "dominant discourse" (1995). It is the language of the educated, the language of the ruling and decision-making class. Those who master this language can influence others and are the least susceptible to being manipulated by those who wield language for unwholesome purposes.

Literacy liberates. Delpit begs us not to water down literacy education for anyone, regardless of their race or social class, because only the truly literate

> have the ability to transform dominant discourses for liberatory purposes. Many who have played significant roles in fighting for the liberation of people of color have done so through the language of the dominant discourse. (1995, p. 163)

Parents know that their children's life chances hang very much on being literate and articulate. They also know that their children must master "the dominant discourses to have access to economic power" (Delpit, 1995, p. 162).

Learning and Earning

Literacy is pivotal to acquiring the type of education that is the path to economic and political power. A recent study in (reputedly class-bound) England found that the ability to read well is the single best indicator of future economic success—regardless of family background (British Broadcasting Corporation News, 2002).

And earnings, as Richard Kahlenberg tells us, "increase lockstep with education" (Kahlenberg, 2004). U.S. census data reveal that those with less than a high school degree earn about $19,000 per year; high school graduates earn an average of $27,000 a year. Those with bachelor's degrees earn $51,000 a year—almost twice that of those with a high school degree. We know, as well, how a college degree confers a level of respect, access, and opportunity beyond earning power. Education, he writes, is "the ticket of entry to the middle class," the key to upward mobility.

One of the saddest features of life in the United States, with its unmatched prosperity, is that 40 percent of those born into the bottom economic fifth stay there as adults (Kahlenberg, 2004). If we want to end this cycle of inequity and intergenerational poverty, education is the surest route. The gateway to a good education is literacy.

But what does it mean to be truly, authentically literate?

6 | Authentic Literacy and Intellectual Development

I'm convinced, after talking with teachers and visiting hundred of classrooms, that literate people can have an incomplete understanding and appreciation of what Allington calls "higher-order literacy" and Vacca calls "advanced levels of literacy." Classroom practice won't change until the case for such literacy is made much more urgently and explicitly in undergraduate and administrative preparation; it must be front and center in our ongoing discussions of how to improve schools. Let's now take a closer, deeper look at literacy—starting with reading.

Deep Reading: The Beginning of an Education

> No subject of study is more important than reading . . . all other
> intellectual powers depend on it.
>
> —Jacques Barzun

Our preoccupation with basic literacy, with decoding and fluency, may be preventing us from helping students to acquire the most important and practical forms of reading—where we read for meaning. James Popham calls it "purposeful reading" (2004, p. 33); Richard Vacca calls it "strategic reading" (2002, p. 6); Deborah Meier calls it "deep reading" (Matthews, 2004, p. 2). To acquire it, students must be given multiple, daily opportunities to read and reread for higher-order purposes—*from the moment they can decode the simplest texts.* Allington suggests that elementary students be invited to consider higher-order questions from the earliest grades. For example, the teacher might ask, "Who would make a better friend: spider or turtle?" as students read or listen to the Ashanti folktale "Hungry Spider and the Turtle" (Allington, 2001, p. 8).

In the next chapter, we'll see why so many students take so long to acquire basic reading fluency. But first let's look at why it is so important to provide students, right from the start, with regular opportunities to read for higher-order intellectual purposes (Allington, 2001).

Strategic Reading

In an aptly named article, "From Efficient Decoders to Strategic Readers," Vacca tells us what we've always known but seldom acted on: that as students read, they must be asked to "decide what's important in a text; synthesize information; draw inferences" (Vacca, 2002, p. 8). All these processes can begin before the 2nd grade.

If you are reading this book, an incalculably rich portion of your education, your current station in life, is a result of "strategic reading." From college on, you read fiction and nonfiction to search for answers and information, weigh evidence, or compare your reading to what you already knew—or to another text. These are complex processes, but they are learned through a fairly straightforward activity: close, purposeful reading—sometimes rereading—with a question or specific purpose in mind.

Close, strategic reading is one of the most powerful and enjoyable ways to develop the ability to think critically and evaluate information—to literally *become smart.* Students should therefore have abundant daily opportunities to carefully read and reread texts for intellectual purposes—and with a pen in hand.

Reading with Pen in Hand

Starting in college, why did so many of us begin to read with a pen or highlighter in hand? Because it helped us focus our minds, isolate, prioritize, and ponder written information to suit our purposes for reading. Sometimes we reread underlined portions of text, looking to detect patterns, gather evidence, evaluate, reconsider, or rebut.

As we did this—make no mistake—our intellects were developing. We were literally learning to manage language and its meaning—the heart of a good education. What makes purposeful reading, pen-in-hand, so important, so life-changing? Some cases:

- I am on an airplane, for the umpteenth time sitting next to someone who is carefully reading a document—pen in hand. The woman is reading several trade journals with titles like *Disease Management.* She tells me that she will be meeting with a team to discuss the relative strengths of their pharmaceuticals against others currently on the market. She is analyzing, evaluating, and then synthesizing (remember Bloom's taxonomy) what she has underlined in order to help team members decide where their company should focus its research and development efforts.

- I've worked with numerous students as young as second grade on reading stories such as *Jack and the Beanstalk.* As they read the story, I have them underline evidence or take notes, which helps them determine if Jack is a great guy—a hero—or on a close or second reading maybe *not* so heroic after all. With stunning consistency, I have seen this activity excite students from 2nd through 12th grade. On a second reading, students invariably see things they hadn't picked up in the first reading. A recent Rand study found that rereading with a purpose is perhaps the most vital strategy for promoting both fluency *and* deep understanding of texts in every discipline (Perkins-Gough, 2002, p. 92). In the debate that ensues, no one is bored, each student can support his opinion from the text, and the discussion leads perfectly into some of the best, most impassioned interpretive or persuasive essays students have ever written. In fact, George Hillocks's landmark research found that students do their best *writing* when it is based on just such text-based *reading* or inquiry (1987).

- My 8th grade daughter and I recently discussed a well-written newspaper opinion piece contributed by a high school student. The writer argues that we shouldn't institute the draft. On a second reading—pen in hand—my daughter began to see that some of the arguments were more logical than others, and that some were just cleverly written opinions.

The woman on the airplane, the 2nd grade students, and my daughter are all engaged in essentially the same simple and yet oh-so-complex activity. They are carefully reading and rereading with a clear, engaging purpose. Then they are thinking analytically and evaluating as they develop their deeper understanding of the text and communicate that orally and in writing. These activities are the essence of true, authentic literacy—of an educated mind.

To paraphrase Deborah Meier, how badly do we want to educate all students? If we are serious, then class time should be spent on this type of reading, thinking, and communicating. Such simple activities would prepare students, from the earliest grades, for their academic, professional, and civic futures. We don't recognize vividly enough that these practices exercise the most relevant intellectual capacities—the ability to detect patterns of meaning and to weigh words and evidence for specific purposes. These "is the stuff of . . ." a trained mind—a learning mind—in action. This approach is both cause and consequence of an intellect that with increasing skill can substantiate, connect, and identify contradictions, and can apply, synthesize, or build on the ideas of others.

In the future, students will need these very capacities as college students, professionals, and contributing members of the voting public. As Barzun sagely asserts, "all other intellectual powers depend on" reading (1991, p. 21). Close, critical, strategic reading—with pen in hand—needs to occupy a substantial portion of every school day.

But strategic reading is not enough. For students to fully develop their intellectual capacities, close reading and rereading must be joined to writing.

The Case for a Writing Revolution

Writing is the litmus paper of thought . . . the very center of schooling.

—Ted Sizer

Writing aids in cognitive development to such an extent that the upper reaches of Bloom's taxonomy could not be reached without the use of some form of writing.

—Bonnie Kuhrt and Pamela Farris

In the same way that we underestimate the importance of close, purposeful reading, we also tend to underestimate how important writing is to intellectual development and career success. Gerald Graff urges us to see that every profession rewards those who are highly competent at

> devising examples that exemplify one's point, generalizing one's conclusions . . . practices that come into play in every field . . . even the most brilliant scientists don't advance in their field unless they can explain to relative non-specialists—in a grant proposal, for example. (2003, p. 22)

Writing equips us for every kind of professional venture; it often determines who gets the grant, the job, or the promotion. According to the National Commission on Writing (2003), headed by former senator Bob Kerrey,

> More than 90 percent of mid-career professionals recently cited the "need to write effectively" as a skill "of great importance" in their day-to-day work. . . . The reward of disciplined writing is the most valuable job attribute of all: a mind equipped to think. (p. 11)

Writing, the commission proclaims, "is not a frill for the few, but an essential skill for the many" (p. 11).

We are witnessing a budding national movement to give writing the serious emphasis it deserves in K–12 education. The SAT and ACT have added a written component to their college entrance exams. Some schools and colleges are starting to base admissions—or entry into the honors track—on how well students write. The National Commission on Writing isn't hesitant to point to what's at stake:

> American education will never realize its potential as an engine of opportunity and economic growth until a writing revolution puts the power of language and communication in their proper place in the classroom. Writing is how students connect the dots in their knowledge. (2003, p. 3)

The value of writing becomes clear only when we understand how it enables students to connect the dots in their knowledge. A deeper look at writing reveals its impact on our ability to learn and think at the highest levels, across the disciplines. Writing literally makes students smarter. We don't hear nearly enough about these benefits in education courses.

Writing and Thinking

Writing, combined with close reading, is among the most valuable, but least understood elements of schooling. Very few teachers have had the chance to consider the real case for writing, or to consider claims like the following:

> If students are to make knowledge their own, they must struggle with the details, wrestle with the facts, and rework raw information and dimly understood concepts into language they can communicate to someone else. In short, *if students are to learn, they must write.* (National Commission on Writing, 2003, p. 9) (emphasis added)

As we've seen, Ted Sizer declares that writing is no less than "the litmus paper of thought" (in Marino, 1998, p. 20). For that reason it should occupy "the very center of schooling" (Marino, 1988, p. 20). To more fully appreciate the central role of writing, consider the reflections of Dennis Sparks, executive director of the National Staff Development Council. Writing, he informs us

> is a way of freezing our thinking, of slowing down the thoughts that pass through our consciousness at lightning speed, so that we can examine our views and alter them if appropriate. Writing enables us to note inconsistencies, logical flaws, and areas that would benefit from additional clarity. (Sparks, 2005, p. 38)

When we write, Sparks is saying, we engage in a singularly close, intense examination of the quality of our own thoughts with respect to logic and clarity. The very act of writing—and revising—teaches us to identify and correct contradictions, to refine and improve and clarify our thoughts—*to think* (Hillocks, 1987). Writing may very well exercise the critical faculties in a way that can't be matched. As the National Commission on Writing tells us, writing "requires students to stretch their minds, sharpen their analytical capabilities, and make valuable and accurate distinctions" (2003, p. 13).

William Zinsser, a widely read authority on the subject, sees writing as "primarily an exercise in logic," that enables us to "write our way" into an understanding of texts or concepts that previously mysti-fied us (1988, p. 14). He urges us to recognize that

> Meaning is *remarkably elusive*. . . . Writing enables us to find out what we know—and what we don't know—about whatever we're trying to learn. Putting an idea into written words is like defrosting the windshield: The idea, so vague out there in the murk, slowly begins to gather itself into a sensible shape . . . all of us know this moment of *finding out what we really want to say by trying in writing to say it.* (pp. 14–16) (emphasis added)

This magical moment, so crucial to our ability to think and process raw knowledge, currently gets hardly a mention in teacher and adminis-trative training. When we help students write and revise, we are help-ing them to create and refine meaning itself, to make connections and see patterns that are at the heart of sophisticated thought. These con-nections lead to insight, invention, and solutions to problems in every realm—social, professional, and political. With reading as its raw material, writing exercises the intellect as it moves from amorphous understanding toward precision and practical application. In the end, writing allows us to discover and produce thought in its clearest and most potent form.

For all our talk about the importance of higher-order thinking, we continue to overlook the fact that writing, linked to close reading, is the workshop of thought—with an almost miraculous effect on stu-dents' critical capacities.

The Miraculous Power of Writing

In "The Learning Power of Writing," R. D. Walshe writes that we "shouldn't hesitate to describe writing as incredible or miraculous . . . a technology which enables thought to operate much more deeply than it normally does during conversation or inward reflection" (1987, p. 22).

Writing allows writers to "contemplate thought . . . until it becomes the best thinking of which they are capable." A "who's who" of linguis-tic heavyweights supports this notion:

• Karl Popper wrote that reading and writing are "the major events in one's intellectual development" (in Walshe, 1987, p. 23).

- Lev Vygotsky, the great Russian educator (who gave us the "Zone of Proximal Development"), lamented that "writing has occupied too narrow a place in school as compared to the enormous role that it plays in children's cultural development" (in Walshe, 1987, p. 23).

- For Kuhrt and Farris, writing is the "means by which students develop metacognitive awareness . . . and thus assume control over it"—control, that is, over the logic and quality of their thoughts. They also write that "the upper reaches of Bloom's taxonomy could not be reached without the use of some form of writing." Writing "facilitates reflection upon the ramifications of an idea and allows for evaluation of a standpoint"—it prevents knee-jerk acceptance of the first thoughts that enter our heads (Kuhrt & Farris, 1990, p. 437).

These higher-level skills do not come naturally; they are learned. As Lisa Ede tells us, until we attempt to write what we learn or read, our thoughts will lack the precision, depth, and clarity that mark first-rate thinking (1987). Those who write have tremendous intellectual advantages over those who don't. As Jacques Barzun observes, the process of writing is the best means for overcoming the mind's natural resistance to logic, order, and precision (1991).

The National Writing Commission speaks volumes with its analysis: "As a nation, we can only imagine how powerful K–16 education might be if writing were put in its proper focus" (National Commission on Writing, 2003, p. 14). Reading and writing, in combination, contribute hugely to critical intelligence. But it is hard to imagine either without the third essential leg of authentic literacy: text-based discussion, dialogue, and argument (close cousins, despite their distinctions).

Importance of Argumentative Literacy

Free human dialogue . . . lies at the heart of education.

—Neil Postman

Gerald Graff speaks for a lot of us when he writes, "Talk—about books and subjects—is as important educationally as are the books and subjects themselves" (2003, p. 9).

Mike Rose, who now teaches at UCLA, agrees:

You could almost define a university education as an initiation
into a variety of powerful ongoing discussions that can occur only
through the repeated use of a new language in the company of others. . . . All students need opportunities to talk about what they're
learning: to test their ideas, reveal their assumptions, talk through
the places where new knowledge clashes with ingrained belief.
(1989, pp. 192–193)

Discussion is indeed an essential part of a university education. But
not, alas, of K–12 education. As the Learning 24/7 study makes clear,
there was evidence of "academic dialog and discussion" in only 0.5
percent of the 1,500 classes they observed (Learning 24/7, 2005).

Despite the importance of academic dialog, most students don't
engage in it until college or later—when people actually judge our
level of "literateness" on how we discuss common texts (Allington,
2001, p. 87). In life and at work, people who read the same text will
naturally and automatically hypothesize, weigh the evidence, and
debate whether the predictions and advice offered in the text seem
adequate and accurate. If the issue is important, we will discuss the
meaning of an important word or phrase and even the perspective of
the writer, looking for bias, especially if the writer is "linked to particular political or advocacy groups." We enthuse about some texts and
"pan others" (2001, pp. 87–89). That is how people talk about texts
outside of school, but in the classroom such discussions don't occur
nearly often enough.

My earliest memory of a high quality *in-school* discussion, which
combined elements of dialogue and argument, was as a high school
senior, visiting my older brother's junior college philosophy class in
the early 1970s. The students were discussing Thoreau's *Civil Disobe-
dience.* I was 17, and I was transfixed. Every student was engaged. The
discussion was fairly orderly, but not without some interruptions and
afterthoughts. This was a small-town junior college, not Yale—and yet
the intellectual energy was palpable. Students hated to see this 75-
minute period end. Many lingered afterward to continue the discussion with the teacher and one another. This environment was sheer

fun, an exciting social arena for thought and the best imaginable way to induce students to engage in close, careful reading for ideas.

School as a Thoughtful Place

Good talk—about books and subjects—stimulates the intellect and is the enemy of boredom, Graff notes (2003, p. 3). It nourishes our critical capacities as it gives kids a chance to try on and test their ideas and viewpoints. And it is fun. As Graff tells us, even children "love to argue" when given an interesting issue (2003, p. 3), and there is no shortage of interesting issues (for ideas, see Appendix A).

In *Horace's School,* Sizer's fatigued, fictional teacher reflects sadly on how school is "not a thoughtful place" but one of boredom and routine (1992, p. 3). Leon Botstein warns how our "failure to challenge the critical faculties of young adolescents can be dangerous" (1997, p. 86). In fact, by postponing students' "intellectual awakening" until college, we ensure that many never will develop an intellectual disposition (Botstein,1997, p. 86). Meier similarly laments that "children are driven into dumbness by our failure to challenge their curiosity" (in Graff, 2003, p. 266).

All of these people are convinced that intellectual exchange in the classroom is an indispensable catalyst for this intellectual awakening to occur. It certainly was for me—but not, unfortunately, in school. Mine began with two friends I met while playing high school football. For reasons I can't remember, we started reading and talking and arguing about editorials and books across the political spectrum. We read and discussed Maugham's *Of Human Bondage,* Huxley's *Brave New World,* and Hesse's *Siddhartha.* We read Haley's *Autobiography of Malcolm X,* Neil Postman, Emerson, Thoreau, William F. Buckley, Charles Reich's provocative *Greening of America*—all on our own. To be fair, we had a few good discussions with one English teacher, one social studies teacher—and had some engaging conversations with our football coach—out of class, during the summer.

We didn't understand everything we read, but we didn't have to. These books and articles were bursting with things to talk about:

Postman had us arguing about the purposes of an education. Reich and Buckley had us thinking, for the first time, about the cultural air we were breathing, about the role of government—and comparing conservative and liberal politics. These texts were packed with provocative issues that we could have been reading and writing and talking about in our English and social studies classes.

One of these friends became a chief executive at two well-known international corporations. When the town newspaper asked him to share high school memories, he mentioned the time we spent walking around in the desert, talking about the books we were reading.

These extracurricular conversations and arguments were vital to our education—perhaps the most enjoyable part. And they prepared us for that university education Mike Rose described as "an initiation into a variety of powerful ongoing discussions" (1989, p. 192).

Once in college, I had the chance to talk and argue endlessly under the guidance of excellent teachers. We spent additional hours talking about books, articles, and ideas in class, over coffee, in our professors' offices—even in their homes. In the charged social and intellectual atmosphere that school can so amply provide, our college classes gave us the chance to read piles of great texts. We got to test our ideas and interpretations on one another in class, to weigh words and phrases we encountered in our reading, to defend and adjust our thinking, to see things from different perspectives—to cultivate those habits of mind that make life richer in every way.

It's a shame that many teachers don't seem to realize that students can participate in such invaluable discussions much earlier than college—2nd grade is an excellent time to begin this intellectual adventure.

Argumentative Literacy: The Soul of an Education

Children in the earliest grades will argue with force and passion, will marshal evidence, and will employ subtlety on behalf of their favorite athletes, pop stars, and automobiles. This is the mind—the intellect—in action. Good academic discourse, Graff points out, is fundamentally the same as good playground polemics. It can be just as fun and engaging—and with undeniable intellectual benefits. For students' sake, we can't afford to be afraid of it. As Graff sees it, we're all better off if we "learn to fight with words rather than with guns and bombs" (2003, p. 4).

A long-time fan of argument in the classroom, even I wasn't quite prepared for the remarkable convergence of opinion around its importance. Graff writes that "argument literacy" is "central to being educated" (2003, p. 3). It grants "access to forms of intellectual capital that have a lot of power in the world" (p. 9). The university itself is largely an entry into an "argumentative culture." Therefore, we should "teach the conflicts" much earlier if we want students to hit the ground running when they arrive at college (p. 13).

Mike Rose defines "critical literacy" itself as "framing an argument or taking someone else's argument apart" (1989, p. 188). This is high-stakes stuff: Lisa Delpit writes of how the underclass suffers immeasurably when we provide a bland, watered-down curriculum that prevents them from acquiring "argumentative literacy," which defines intellectual maturity and prepares us for adult life (in Graff, 2003, p. 36). Neil Postman regards argument as the soul of an education, and its justification—the very "reason for schooling: to provide our youth with the knowledge and will to participate in the great experiment; to teach them *how to argue* and to help them discover what questions are worth arguing about" (1997, p. 73) (emphasis added).

Christopher Lasch, the late social commentator, avers that information means nothing until we "get into arguments that focus and fully engage our attention" (1995, p.163). Like Postman, he is emphatic that argument not only forms "the essence of education" but (we'll get to this) prepares a democratic society for self-governance. In a chapter entitled "The Lost Art of Argument," he writes that only argument, written and oral, can fully "cultivate the virtues of eloquence, clarity of thought and expression, and sound judgment" (pp. 170–171). After all,

> It is only by subjecting our preferences and projects to the test of debate that we come to understand what we know and what we still need to learn. Until we have to defend our opinions in public, they remain opinions . . . half-formed convictions based on random impressions and unexamined assumptions. It is the act of articulating and defending our views that lifts them out of the category of "opinions," gives them shape and definition and makes it possible

for others to recognize them as a description of their own experience as well. In short, we come to know our own minds only by
explaining ourselves to others. (p. 171)

Please note the parallels between these remarks about argument and
those we have seen about the benefits of writing. Lasch goes on to say
that both oral and written arguments are vital to examining, discover-
ing, and refining what we think and know. The quality of our writing
and discussion is, in turn, a function of how well—how deeply and
carefully—we read. Generous amounts of reading, writing, and argument all are essential to the development of truly literate and educated students.

Argumentative Illiteracy

Because argument is at the heart of intellectual development and
maturity, it is lamentable, as Graff notes, that only about 20 percent of
students—of those who make it to college, mind you—are truly ready
for this adventure (2003, p. 3). This lack of preparation delays and prevents them, during their precious college years, from reaching their
maximum intellectual and professional potential. K–12 education
doesn't prepare them for this argumentative culture: Only consider the
findings of a study on students' abilities to analyze text: fully two-thirds
of students at a prestigious university couldn't detect the most flagrant
contradictions in a text that was purposely laced with them. The study
concludes that schools do very little to enhance students' critical reading capacities. On the contrary, students are (this is ominous) "trained
to accept the word of experts at face value" (Graff, p. 68). As Postman writes, anyone can manipulate a populace that can't distinguish
between facts and inferences, a population from whom we don't need
to conceal contradictions (1988, pp. 90–91). Surely this statistic should
awaken us to the consequences of prevailing instructional practices
that leave so little room for critical and argumentative literacy.

    Discussion—talk about books and other texts—is where students
develop this argumentative literacy and an appreciation for the power
of ideas, including their own. It is where we come to see their consequences and import in the public, social sphere—and the impact they

have on people and institutions. There will never be a substitute. For Dewey, reading and writing, as important as they are, don't replace the need for the "vital and outgoing thought and emotion" of "face to face dialogue" (in Lasch, 1995, p. 172). This type of interaction on issues of importance excites students' interest in English, science, social studies, and beyond—especially when linked to meaningful controversy.

And no idea is without controversy. As Postman points out, everything we know *is the result of questions,* of someone contesting the veracity or hidden implications of established "facts" or arguments.

Thought and Emotion in East Harlem

Discussion and argument are central to developing those habits of mind Deborah Meier emphasizes at her schools. I once visited Central Park East Secondary School in East Harlem, when Meier was still the principal there. Intellectual argument was a daily feature of life at her school. For Meier, argument and discussion provide perhaps the best opportunity for kids to become critical thinkers, for us to help them see "the power of their ideas" (the title of Meier's 2002 book).

I'll never forget a discussion by a group of mostly minority 8th graders at Central Park East. The young Latino teacher raised an issue that had emerged in a story students had read: whether it was appropriate for blacks or non-blacks to use the "n" word in jest. A melee ensued. After a raucous start, the teacher restored order, and students offered all kinds of arguments for and against, referring to the text, listening and responding to each other's points—she made sure of this. Clichés gave way to occasional silence, then to more measured, thoughtful opinions. Such rich and productive discussion was a regular part of life at Central Park East, where high proportions of poor and minority students went on to attend and graduate from the most prestigious colleges in the land.

I wish such discussion were a regular feature in more schools, including the schools my daughters have attended. Given a good text, an arresting issue, students like to argue, in small groups or as a class. We're daft if we don't see that argument teaches them to think and is about the best inducement we have for getting them to read purposefully and write with passion and energy—*in class,* where they can feel the energy of one another's ideas and worldviews. Innumerable texts address controversies that can enliven subject matter as they help students to cultivate precision, clarity, and a respect for logic and evidence.

Reading, writing, and discussion—these three[1]—are the foundation for a well-equipped mind: the key to equity, access, and economic opportunity. They will mightily promote achievement gains even as they help to make school, in Ted Sizer's phrase, a "thoughtful place"— a more relevant, interesting, and therefore educational place for our children to spend their precious school years. We need to begin making the case that these activities truly prepare students for every aspect of life, for the life of the mind—and for civic participation, which may be literacy's highest good.

Literacy and Democracy

> If we insist on argument as the essence of education, we will defend democracy...as the most educational form of government.
>
> —Christopher Lasch

We have looked at several important reasons to promote authentic literacy in schools: to combat boredom and to promote equity, college access, and economic opportunity. But there is another, equally important reason for these major changes in what and how we teach. Neil Postman refers to it as the "American Experiment" or "project"; it is the never-finished pursuit, through learning and argument, of the ideals we enshrine—liberty, fairness, and equal opportunity (1997).

This is a moral project. It is also an intellectual project. Our success, according to Postman, Lasch, Dewey, and others, will depend on our ability to read, to listen and to argue—well, reasonably, and fairly—as we engage the issues of the day. Free access to information is essential, but no more important than the intellectual capacity to make sense of that information: to think, discern, and make distinctions that inform our conversations, our decisions, how we vote. Schools are in the best possible position to foster this thoughtful disposition so essential to democracy.

The truth and importance of this role is implicit in Thomas Jefferson's argument, as one of the earliest advocates of public education, for a system of schools that would promote "informed discretion"—a bedrock necessity for a healthy electorate. Dewey also supported this role, arguing that democracy itself requires that we make ample room in the school day for "systematic inquiry" and "dialogue" (Lasch, 1995, p. 172). Postman warns that anyone can manipulate a population that can't discern overgeneralizations or logical flaws in arguments. He cites H. G. Wells's assertion that "civilization is in a race between education and disaster" and that only effective "language education" can rescue us from prejudice and provinciality (1988, pp. 20–21). George Orwell wrote that no nation could be both "ignorant and free." Ignorance, contradiction, and prejudice surround us, but schools can liberate us from these, far better than they currently do.

In civic terms, we get what we pay for. These observations point to the relationship between wise government and a thoughtful, discriminating public—a public that has learned how to weigh words and evidence, and compare the relative strengths of arguments and counter-arguments.

We have a long way to go. Consider, for instance, the nature of political debate among both average citizens and political leaders. Instead of listening carefully to one another's arguments to learn in ways that will "strengthen civil society," they engage in political debate that "consists largely of ideological slogans endlessly repeated to audiences composed mainly of the party faithful" (Lasch, 1995, p. 101).

Political campaigns are built around endless, artful repetition of poll-tested slogans that stop honest argument. They aren't intended to provoke thought or persuade; they are often intended to appeal viscerally, not rationally, to the entrenched opinions and unexamined prejudices of "the party faithful." But as Lasch and others point out, to solve our increasingly complex problems, "fresh thinking is desperately needed" (p. 101). Our last presidential election convinced me that many people declare their allegiances before they ever consider different sides of the most complex issues we face. We aren't interested in hearing or reading about the ideas of those in different camps, which might cause us to detect contradictions or to temper or rethink our opinions. Instead of, say, reading both sides of an issue in the op-ed pages and respectfully exchanging claims and counterclaims with others, we bypass this process entirely; too many prefer to take comfort in these endlessly repeated slogans.

Some observers are calling for change. In his regular *Newsweek* column, Fareed Zakaria writes about the October 2004 dust-up on MSNBC's *Crossfire*. The guest was comedian Jon Stewart, who broke protocol and tore into Tucker Carlson and Paul Begala, telling them that programs like theirs are "hurting America." Such shows, Stewart insisted, are not forums for reasoned argument but mere "theater" where each side defends its camp with thoughtless, lockstep consistency. The hosts were aghast.

But Stewart was right. The "structure for political life," writes Zakaria, "is increasingly made for theater . . . but not for governing" (2004, p. 21).

A more literate populace won't abide such nonsense. It will have a lower tolerance for stupid, distorted political talk and advertisements, a growing appreciation for clarity and accuracy. Such a people will know that all sides—including "our" side—will resort to exaggeration and propaganda and that we must hold them as accountable as those we traditionally oppose.

We have *12 years* to cultivate such a disposition, to provide hundreds of opportunities for students to read, think, discuss, question, and write in a more intellectually charged classroom. Nothing but good will come of this.

In this crucial area of literacy, the civic, economic, and moral stakes are exceedingly high, and the potential is incalculable. For this reason, we have to look, unblinkingly, at the brutal facts about literacy education. The best news is that this close look at literacy reveals how some fairly simple actions and changes could result in rapid, meaningful advances in authentic literacy, with manifold benefits.

Note

1. I have not mentioned the teaching of vocabulary, but I do believe it deserves a place in the curriculum and is part of reading for meaning. Although "direct" teaching is often maligned, teaching a certain amount of selected vocabulary

enlarges our ability to understand texts of increasing complexity as it increases our knowledge of essential concepts. Vocabulary instruction also has a significant impact on achievement levels. New words open up the world for students at every level. An excellent, readable treatment of this subject—with proven, practical strategies—is Robert Marzano's *Building Background Knowledge for Academic Achievement* (2004).

7 The Startling State of Literacy Education

Startling as this may sound, the truth is that many children read for a remarkably small percentage of the school day.

—Lucy McCormick Calkins

Almost every high school kid can decode, but many can't read with higher-order comprehension. So: we put them in courses where they read very little—and aren't required to read with higher-order comprehension.

—Gene Bottoms

We've seen how literacy, rightly understood and acquired, changes lives. It affects our ability to think, to reason, to speak, and to govern. In this chapter, however, we will see that current practice is very much at odds with the best we know about helping students to become authentically literate. Literacy instruction, like medical practice at the time of the Flexner report, presents us with a supreme opportunity for the general improvement of schooling.

I have asked numerous audiences in dozens of states the following question: What two activities are least apt to occur during a typical English or language arts class?

In every case, after a quiet moment, come the answers, one then the other:

"Reading."

"Writing."

Heads nod; there is some nervous laughter. I always ask the audience if something so counterintuitive could really be true. I get lots of uncomfortable acknowledgments. I then ask if this lack of reading and writing could possibly be good for kids. Lots of scattered responses: "no."

I ask a few more related questions. What do we know about the nature of most reading assignments and class discussions? Are they typically lower-order, focused on facts and recall; or higher-order, focused on interpretive, open-ended discussions? The answer is loud and immediate: "lower-order."

I then ask them: have you, since you attended college, done a lot of reading, for different purposes, with a pen or highlighter in hand? A loud, affirmative response. Is such purposeful reading, pen in hand, an almost universal way that we engage in deep reading and critical reasoning? Absolutely. Should our students, from the earliest grades, be given interpretive prompts or purposes *before* they read, to guide their reading, pen-in-hand, on a daily basis? Should teachers regularly select short passages and carefully explain their thoughts as they analyze and make meaning of the words and sentences, so that students can see how adults tackle text? "Of course," the audience members respond.

I ask questions about writing: should students receive clear, detailed instruction—entire lessons—on each respective element of a writing rubric? And isn't repeated teacher modeling accompanied by exemplars of good written work essential to understanding these criteria of good writing? And shouldn't students be taught—very carefully and thoroughly—to evaluate their own written work with these rubrics (a practice that saves teachers time and is good pedagogy)? No arguments; nearly everyone knows and agrees with all of these excellent, widely known practices.

Then comes the kicker: how routinely do such practices—purposeful reading and interpretive modeling or "think-alouds," and frequent writing instruction focusing on only one criterion in a scoring guide—actually occur in the average classroom? There is almost always some laughter. Even now, in the age of accountability, the sum of their responses is: rarely, if at all, in most classrooms. There are exceptions, of course.

I ask them, as I now ask you, to let these realizations sink in. Not because these facts are depressing, but because they point so conclusively to how simple, immediate actions could make an astonishing difference in the quality of our schools. Improvements here—which are hardly out of reach—would be felt profoundly in *every subject* where students benefit from being good thinkers, readers, and writers.

The irony is that that while the most effective reading and writing instruction is still relatively rare, we talk as though underachievement and underdeveloped critical reasoning capacities are the result of mysterious or insurmountable social or fiscal factors. But these factors are not, in the main, the ones that keep kids down. They are a result of unfortunate practices that crept into schools and were allowed to stay there. Please indulge me as I share evidence from personal experience, and then—very importantly—from the best research that roundly confirms my observations.

The Education of an English Teacher

I am grateful that as an English major in college, most of the instruction I received was quite good; some was excellent. It mostly consisted of reading, writing, and exchanging opinions about the ideas and characters in the books we read.

There were bumps in the road; I came to college having received mostly *As* on written assignments, thinking I wrote well. A handful of my professors disabused me of that notion and helped me to become a better writer. I am forever indebted to them.

It wasn't until my senior year in college that I had my first disturbing encounter with the culture of "English education"—something quite different from the reading, writing, and discussion I thought was the essence of literacy.

In my "English teaching methods" course, I remember feeling increasingly uneasy: what we were learning in the class seemed to have very little connection to literacy: to learning to read, write, or think well.

Authentic Literacy vs. "Stuff"

If Mike Rose's teacher, Jack MacFarland, had spent time in my methods course, he might have thought he was on an alien planet. We never talked about how to teach students to read purposefully or how to develop enticing questions that could guide student reading or discussion. We weren't taught to teach or evaluate student writing. The essential purpose and intellectually enlarging power of writing and revising, described in the previous chapter, were never mentioned.

Instead, we learned to devise lessons full of short, diverting activities and worksheets. "Multimedia" experiences, such as filmstrips and movies, were strongly encouraged, with no discussion of their intellectual advantages or disadvantages. We assembled individualized, theme-based learning kits, with hands-on or artistic activities, crossword puzzles, and games. Those who created the most elaborate, quasi-artistic activities received lavish praise for their efforts. Serious attention was given to bulletin board design.

It was only too clear that reading and writing were subordinate to such activities. Evidently, tackling the issues and the use of language—of potent words or phrases in a text—were too serious or boring for most students. Diverting, hands-on activities were the real coin of the realm. Weeks of nonliterary activities would be built around the reading of a single short story or novel. *The teaching of writing and close, critical reading was never mentioned.*

Anticipating my student teaching, I felt a kind of dread. I knew that the only way I could teach English was by doing my best to help my students, as Mike Rose writes, to "read and talk and write their way toward understanding" (1989, p. 146). I hoped I could get away with it.

Student Teaching

No such luck. My worst fears were confirmed as I ran head-on into the most depressing feature of language arts: a relative indifference to substantive reading, writing, and discussion about texts. I worked with several industrious, highly regarded teachers. But most of them had been infected (as I eventually was) by the same disease. The smallest portion of class time was spent reading, and even less time was spent writing. Text-based discussion was brief and focused mostly on facts. Most of it, as Allington observes, was "shallow and barren" (2001 p. 89). Teachers weren't encouraged to take discussion, or preparation for it, seriously. A staggering proportion of daily lessons, often painstakingly planned, consisted of nonliterary, time-filling activities: filmstrips, movies, worksheets, time spent at "centers," and the perennial emphasis on irrelevant literary terms. Students drew pictures and colored and made things from fabric and butcher paper. Days were devoted to making elaborate book covers ("publishing" was the rage) for written work that had been completed in mere minutes *and in one draft*—with no explicit criteria for evaluating its quality. All these activities received high praise from administrators—and, to my amazement, from local education professors.

For the first eight weeks of my student teaching, I was given complete freedom (no guidance whatsoever) to teach a unit on Dickens. In that time, I had the students read three novels, both in class and for homework. I gave short pop quizzes to make sure they were doing the required reading. We learned lots of vocabulary and discussed the ideas in the assigned reading almost daily, from questions I carefully prepared for each chapter.

In this eight-week period, I taught them to organize and write three critical essays in two drafts each, about each of the novels. I had them write the papers in stages, much of it during class, so that they could consult with me and so that the paper load wasn't overwhelming. Final copies were generally easy to grade because problems had been corrected in earlier drafts and stages.

At the end of my stint, I received a letter, signed by dozens of students, telling me how much they had enjoyed the eight weeks. Not so my supervising teacher, a smart, hard-working veteran. He waited until nearly the end of the eight weeks to tell me that he was very disappointed: that I wasn't the least bit—I'll never forget the word— "creative." I taught "as though this were a college class."

My First Teaching Job

I should have known something was awry when I was asked, as a first-year teacher, to help another teacher write the curriculum. In two days. For "accreditation." Our irrelevant, hastily written curriculum was submitted and passed with flying colors. I don't believe anyone—teacher or administrator—ever looked at it or had to (let *that* sink in).

I eventually taught middle and high school English in three schools. At two of them, I discovered that no one would ever ask me what I taught or how often; that most of my colleagues did not teach writing; that the typical amounts of required reading were scant in the extreme. At two of these schools, I came to know several dedicated Title I teachers whose students, I was to find out, seldom actually read. A couple of them were proud to tell me that they insisted that students "read for 10 minutes a day." In one school, my English department head suggested that I simply teach grammar exercises—every day—throughout the first semester (from Warriner's *English Composition and Grammar*). Then, during second semester, I was to teach a story a week (a 20- or 30-minute read) from the basal. When I asked about writing, she said something like, "With 140 students? Are you kidding?"

The View from the Central Office: A Ray of Hope

Years later, I found myself, almost accidentally, at the central office in a district whose schools had received several prestigious awards. The superintendent and I discovered that we were both keen on the value of writing. But neither of us had the foggiest notion of whether or how well writing was being taught in our schools. He had me ask around. Several awkward interviews later, I found that no one else knew if or how well writing was being taught. One English department chair (at a school that had just received the state's most prestigious award) told me that she did not teach writing and did not expect her teachers to do so either. After all, she said, computer programs were being developed that would virtually do the writing for us.

There was one glorious exception: a team of teachers who evidently hadn't learned that writing was irrelevant or too time-consuming to teach. At the beginning of the second semester, they began to have their students read and discuss articles on controversial topics and then write persuasive essays from their readings of these texts (the very kind of reading and writing that George Hillocks found to be the best way to promote high-quality writing; see Hillocks, 1987). The teachers used the state writing rubric to guide their teaching and students' self-assessment efforts. I dropped by one day just after they had scored a set of essays. They were pleased to tell me that "all" of their students had written effective papers. I tried, tactfully, to ask them if they were sure about these results (almost half their students were receiving free and reduced-price lunches). They clearly didn't appreciate my question and invited me to read some of the lowest-scoring of these student papers. To my amazement, every paper was well-written by any 8th grade standard.

For those who assume that there is nothing unusual about such instruction, consider the impact of this single semester of team-based effort to provide frequent, intensive opportunities for students to read, discuss, and write about the controversial issues they encountered in various texts. Logic would dictate that if most teachers already taught in this manner—more or less—there wouldn't be much effect. But an effect there was: their students' scores on the state writing assessment, which so many critics were openly vilifying as a poor measure of "real" writing, rose from the state average to a three-way tie for first place in the state. Neither of the two schools with which they tied had any students receiving free or reduced-price lunch.

These were two excellent teachers, but their improvements made clear that effective writing instruction was very much within our reach—but rare. Was the problem restricted to their region or state? Apparently not.

The View from the University

Both before and during my secondary teaching stints, I had the chance to teach freshman English to students at a large state university. About half of the students who attended there came from out of state, from all parts of the country—something of a national sample. Most of the students came from middle and upper-class families and schools.

But their writing, we English teachers agreed, was quite poor. It became obvious that these students had done very little expository or persuasive writing and had received almost no real *instruction* in how to write. The pattern was indisputable: most of them, from various states and places, had attended schools situated in fairly privileged settings. But they had written no more than an occasional story or book report, usually in one draft. In general, they received very little feedback and no opportunity for revision. Yet they had received very high grades on these infrequent assignments.

For these students, almost half of whom would drop out of college, writing and writing instruction had been grossly neglected. What about reading?

The Incredible Lightness of Reading

When my nephew was in the 8th grade, he was given an ultimatum: pass English in summer school or don't move on to high school. My sister asked me to meet with his teacher to see what we could do to make sure he succeeded.

When I asked the veteran teacher what books or novels they would be reading, she said that they would be reading "a novel": *Do Bananas Chew Gum* (she hadn't read it yet). It is a 5th grade novel. Even a very slow, early grade reader could bang it out in just a few class periods. When I asked what they would be writing, she became visibly uncomfortable and said that there wouldn't be any time for written assignments as this course would focus on "the basics"—whatever that meant.

I asked her if, as an alternative, I could supervise an independent study for my nephew, which she gladly agreed to. I had to clear it with the principal, who was also agreeable but didn't see anything odd about receiving full credit for 8th grade English in a course where students would read only one upper-elementary grade novel and write no papers.

My own children's education strongly conforms to this same pattern. At the time of this writing, they are in the 8th and 9th grade, respectively. They have attended school in three school systems, each school carefully selected. With very few exceptions, the amount and quality of in-class reading, especially purposeful reading, has been minimal in the extreme.

With a few happy exceptions, they have rarely been asked, much less taught, to engage in "strategic reading"—to read for an intellectual or arresting purpose. In the main, they haven't received explicit instruction in how to underline or take notes or reread portions of text in order to support an interpretation or identify patterns of meaning for purposes of discussion or writing. Years have passed without their being taught to write and self-evaluate their writing with the aid of a rubric. Even during testing years, and in "honors" courses, they haven't been given an explanation of the elements in the state writing rubric. Most of their teachers openly expressed their belief that rubrics merely stifle "creativity." Some of my daughters' most high-stakes written assignments had to be written and proofread in one draft, in a single period, on a topic they weren't given until the day of the assignment, with no opportunity to revise or rewrite.

Like a lot of people, I have been blessed with smart, conscientious children. They will likely graduate from college. But how much better off would they be, academically and intellectually, if they had been given daily opportunities to read and discuss texts, if they had frequent opportunities to discover and interpret and wrestle with ideas on paper? What doors would open, what career options, what intellectual adventures might await them?

The View from Hundreds of Classrooms

If students weren't doing much reading or writing, what *were* they doing? I was about to find out.

I was invited to tour an award-winning school with educators from around the country on an obvious "showcase day." What I saw, up close, during language arts was deeply unsettling. In every class we visited, most students were engaged in activities that had nothing to do with literacy.

To my surprise, in the lunchtime discussion that followed the tour, there was only unqualified praise from each of the other visitors. Most were education professors and high-ranking school administrators. I couldn't help myself: I asked if anyone had noticed that most of what we saw in classrooms—during the reading and language arts block—had nothing to do with the ability to read or write. Most of the students, in most of the classrooms, were coloring—or drawing, cutting, or pasting. Some chatted quietly, while the teacher worked in one corner of the room with a small group.

The responses from the other guests ran from interested to offended—but not one of them, including the school's principal, denied what we had seen.

I then asked if the lack of reading and writing might explain why this high-poverty (if award-winning) school hadn't realized any achievement gains, despite the school's huge infusion of time and funding? Some of the guests became very quiet; a few said the usual stuff about test scores being meaningless. But no one denied that these poor students, so desperately in need of literacy skills, were engaged in activities with very little educational value.

A Defining Moment

This was a defining moment for me: what if this situation wasn't rare, but fairly common? This experience emboldened me to begin asking clients if we could tour classrooms together, especially during reading or language arts. I assured them that we wouldn't be looking for individual teachers' shortcomings but only for patterns of good or poor instruction. We were always joined by a teacher or two. We focused on two questions:

- Did the activity have anything to do with literacy; with learning to read or write?

- How many students were clearly engaged—were on task?

As I mentioned in Chapter 1, these tours were an epiphany for all of us. In hundreds of classrooms in a number of states, there was a consistent pattern—even in high-scoring schools: the majority of lessons lacked the most fundamental elements of good instruction. The learning outcome was seldom clear to us or to students; the nature of instruction allowed many, if not most students to tune out—right up through middle and high school.

In the lowest-achieving schools, where students didn't know the alphabet and couldn't decode even simple texts, most of the reading period was spent on activities such as drawing and coloring or filling in worksheets that had no connection to important learning outcomes. Students were often given 30 or 40 minutes to finish worksheets that could have been completed in minutes. Even in the small, "guided reading" groups, the work itself was often poorly organized.

Eventually, it became apparent that student assessment was surprisingly rare and haphazard. Students would spend days, even weeks, on activities without being assessed. A surprising proportion of student work was handed in but never returned—or returned weeks later, often without written feedback, and with no chance to revise.

Teachers have lately been required to conduct exhaustive, student-by-student reading assessments that can take days to conduct. But few are told how to use their results. We never encountered a single case where teachers used these assessment results *to adjust or improve instruction;* they used them to group or regroup students.

In every kind of school, from poor to affluent, we seldom caught kids reading or writing. We had the same findings as the Learning 24/7 classroom observation study (Learning 24/7, 2005): we saw no writing instruction, no instruction in the elements of a writing rubric, no modeling, no use of writing exemplars. What we did see was staggering amounts of coloring. We were not alone.

The Crayola Curriculum

Others were seeing the same things in classrooms across the country. Writer and consultant Doug Reeves was similarly dismayed by the amount of time students spent "coloring, cutting, and pasting." Superintendent Joyce Bales, mentioned earlier for her accomplishments in

Pueblo, Colorado, schools, had begun to visit classrooms regularly. I attended a meeting in which she had to point out that she was still seeing far too much coloring and pasting on her rounds. Finally, I heard Kati Haycock of the Education Trust describe the plight of students who lack access to a good education. Then she paused and in sobering tones described the discovery she and her research team had made—that coloring was *the single most predominant activity* in the schools they had observed—right up through middle school.

With some trepidation, I decided to test this message on a wider public and wrote of this experience in a piece for *Education Week*. I entitled it "The Crayola Curriculum" (Schmoker, 2001a).

I waited for an onslaught of negative opinion. It never came. Not a single response contradicted the basic facts. Instead, teachers, administrators, and consultants sent me a record number of e-mails saying they had seen or suspected these patterns for years.

To cite only a few:

• One educator wrote that "Your article hit my mail ring like a bolt of lightning. . . . There are a lot of teachers out there saying 'Thank you for noticing that the kids aren't reading and writing and the emperor has no clothes.'"

• A newspaper reporter in northern California wrote that it confirmed his perception of what he was seeing in schools and classrooms—that only about one-fourth of language arts instruction was meaningful.

• A middle school teacher sent me a note thanking me for "vindicating a long-held suspicion" about literacy instruction.

• A former principal wrote to me lamenting the "lack of engagement . . . meaningless activities—all in the name of education."

• Of particular interest: a long-time teacher and former colleague wrote to me from the leading-edge school district where we had worked together. Now a district trainer, she had spent many hours in classrooms. She nonetheless wrote that "I couldn't be more in agreement with your findings, no matter how depressing."

- A 30-year veteran teacher wrote that the article was "right-on, but sad." He compared the use of class time to poor coaching activities, where players spend most of their time merely waiting and chatting with their teammates.

- My friend, writer and speaker Harry Wong, sent the piece out on his e-newsletter, as he had seen these same tendencies in schools. (He suggested we all buy Crayola stock.)

- Carol Jago, a highly-respected author and high school English teacher in Santa Monica, California, wrote to tell me that coloring was rife *even up through high school.*

No one—not a soul—disagreed with these perceptions. I even tested them, point by point, on a union head who had spent time in classrooms. He agreed with every point.

Despite the seemingly untouchable nature of this issue, district office administrators continue to tell me that they have shared this piece with their teaching staffs. None have ever told me that it was met with anger or disagreement.

Enough. If you suspect that these perceptions are selective or anecdotal, tour your own schools; there is no substitute for this experience. And also consider what some of our best and most admired researchers have to say about the state of literacy instruction in America.

The State of Literary Education: What Researchers Say

The research pointing to the sad, startling state of literacy instruction has a long and established pedigree.

English: Lost and Confused

English—or language arts—lost its way some time ago. In *Anti-Intellectualism in American Life,* Richard Hofstadter outlines education's merciless march, starting in the early 1900s, against the "the development of intellectual capacity" (1962, p. 335). Serious reading and writing were the first casualties, as English devolved into any activity that could be vaguely deemed "communication skills" (p. 347).

Judith Warren Little found that the substance of what was taught in English classes varied greatly from teacher to teacher. The differences among teachers were so considerable that she concluded that it made no sense to refer to this incoherent hodge-podge by the same name—"English" (Little, 1990). No "guaranteed and viable curriculum" here.

This view is not extreme; Little is greatly respected in the research community. A similarly well-known and respected school reformer, Ted Sizer, spent considerable time in high school English classes. He too concludes that "English teachers can't decide what their subject really is" (1992, p. 7).

What is the upshot of such incoherence? In most schools, English is among students' least favorite subjects. But in classes where reading and writing engage the mind and are "catalysts for inquiry," English rises to *the top of the list.* Unfortunately, as Goodlad's studies show, almost all of what goes on in English emphasizes only "recall or recognition." He found that most students endured English classes where they "rarely read or wrote . . . they scarcely even speculated on meanings, discussed alternative interpretations" of what they did read (in Marino, 1998, pp.19–20).

These findings echo Hofstadter's dark conclusions about "anti-intellectualism" in America, and Powell, Farrar, and Cohen's observation that there is a shocking indifference, a "wholesale absence of intensity about thinking" in our curriculum (1985, p. 103).

This research by Little, Sizer, and Goodlad primarily concerns literacy instruction at the secondary level, which we'll return to. But let's look first at what research says about the high-stakes early grades, where these trends begin and where a child's future can be made or broken.

The Unintended Consequences of Guided Reading

As we've seen, the drift from authentic reading, writing, and talking starts in the earliest grades.

The popular, perhaps predominant model is for small groups of students to take their turn spending a short but intensive session with the teacher. This approach can be very effective for those in the small group, but only if the work is carefully sequenced, quickly paced, and well-organized—suffused with urgency to ensure that students are meeting clear expectations on a sensibly paced schedule. However, we've seen tremendous inconsistency with respect to all of these factors—which (once again) aren't monitored.

But the larger question is: what are most students doing while the teacher works with the small group? The answer is: not much.

This situation has to be one of the most disturbing, if overlooked actualities in all of K–12 education (and in some places it is beginning to change). We know the enormous importance of time-on-task, of how achievement hinges so much on the most efficient use of class time—which has seldom been spent wisely (Wahlberg, 1988; Berliner, 1984; Haycock, 2005). We are lately inundated with articles that urge longer school days and extended reading periods or lament the additional time spent on state-tested areas like reading—at the expense of enrichment or the arts.

We must see the irony here, because in many schools, we are squandering about two-thirds of the reading period. Used wisely, this time would be enough to promote unprecedented levels of success in literacy *without reducing arts and enrichment activities.*

This observation isn't based on hearsay. Elmore found this same pattern in his visits to classrooms. Teachers were so focused on the small groups that they weren't aware that most students, most of the time, were engaged in meaningless activities. Students couldn't even tell him what they were learning or why (2005). Ford and Opitz speak for most researchers when they point out that despite the value of small-group work, the research leaves the most pertinent questions

> unanswered about what the other children should be doing and the quality of the instruction when they are away from the teacher . . . [as] approximately two-thirds of a student's time during the designated reading block would be spent away from the teacher (2002, pp. 710–711).

What are students doing with this precious two-thirds of class time? They are "independently engaged in a menu of *cut, color, and paste* response projects" (p. 711) (emphasis added).

Ford and Opitz's conclusion—and they are advocates (as I am) of effective guided reading—is that students receive less benefit from small group work than in the traditional, whole-class model.

There is still hope here. Researchers are starting to be more candid and forthright about where we have gone wrong; this candor is the beginning of improvement. Let's look at some other prominent researchers whose courage and candor can break us out of our funk in the area of literacy education.

Literature-Based Arts and Crafts

The guided reading model isn't the only problem; even with whole-class instruction, the lack of quality control works against effective or consistent implementation of the (presumably) same reading program or curriculum. I have found, for instance, that almost anything can be done in the name of "whole language" or "reading workshop." I'm not disparaging the best elements of these approaches. But when no one monitors to ensure a focus on the best standards taught at an effective pace, these approaches devolve all too easily into low expectations and minimal amounts of actual reading and writing.

With all of these approaches, the common problem has to do with how class time is squandered. Elaine McEwan, a well-known laborer in this field, describes elementary school students who spent 37 hours—the equivalent of an entire month of language arts—building a papier-mâché dinosaur. "Those kids," writes McEwan, "couldn't read well, but they spent all that time messing with chicken wire and wheat paste." School leaders were so proud of this activity that they made sure it was featured in the local newspaper (in Vail, 2001, p. 4).

Lucy McCormick Calkins is among the most respected names in literacy education. She notices the same patterns, the frequency with which "there is no reading in the reading curriculum." There is the same note of dismay in her observation that

> Startling as this may sound, the truth is that many children read for a remarkably small percentage of the school day . . . children

> sometimes spend two and a half hours a day in reading instruction and only ten minutes of that time actually reading. (Calkins, Montgomery, & Santman, 1998, pp. 51–52)

Instead of reading, children spend large portions of their reading period on what Calkins calls "literature-based arts and crafts"—activities such as "making dioramas, game boards, posters, or mobiles to accompany a book . . . making new books with illustrations . . . murals or other artwork" (p. 51). Such findings certainly take much of the mystery out of poor reading performance and the achievement gap.

And these activities do not occur just in the elementary grades. When researcher Ruth Mitchell toured schools, she found high school English students who seldom read or wrote. They were too busy drawing and coloring for projects such as shields that represented Greek gods or goddesses. On another trip to two Midwestern high schools, she found only 1 of 8 assignments was at grade level. A colleague of hers then visited 40 English classes—but found only one class in which appropriate learning was going on (2004, p. A21).

Such "stuff" as Richard Allington calls it, has been typical fare in my daughters' language arts classrooms over the years. Compare Calkins's list to the options one of my daughters was given to demonstrate, of all things, her understanding of a novel:

- A diorama (a miniature stage set with dolls or characters)

- An illustrated map

- A book jacket

- A movie poster

- A 3-D mobile

This assignment was for *honors* English and was justified, as I've heard many teachers aver, in the name of "creativity." I'm reminded of Barzun's reference to how "that prostituted word, 'creative,'" has justified so much mindless activity (1991, p. 106). That year, a state testing year, my daughter was never taught how to write and was never taught the state writing criteria. She was never given a single sample of a well-written expository essay for analysis—even though the state provides these.

In the area of reading, where the state assessment and study materials give emphatic weight to higher-order, analytic reading, my daughters never received instruction on how to infer or interpret, to comb through a text to support assertions with evidence, or to analyze an author's purpose or bias (all skills prominently featured in the state assessment guide). She did, however spend months of class time on what can only be called "literature-based arts and crafts."

The Dismal Research on Writing

Despite the crucial role that writing plays in intellectual development and future success, the research paints a discouraging picture. Researchers Kameenui and Carnine have found that studies concur that there is very little writing instruction in our schools, K–12 (1998, p. 72). As researcher Claudia Gentile concludes, "We can't expect students to produce excellent, complicated, effective writing if they're receiving little instruction in it" (in Jones, 1995, p. 22).

Writing is seldom assigned and even more rarely taught. A study by the American Federation of Teachers found that "writing never gets the attention it deserves" (Jones, 1995, p. 22). The associate director of the National Council of Teachers of English once lamented that there is "a lot of publicity" about writing, but "not as much writing going on as people think" (Jones, 1995, p. 18).

An important research project confirms what many have known for decades—that even the college-bound can't write and haven't been taught to write. Standards for Success is a joint effort by the Association of American Universities, the Pew Charitable Trusts, and Oregon's Center for Policy Research. Their in-depth study is based on interviews with hundreds of university faculty members, analyses of high school and college syllabi, and samples of college-level assignments. The evidence points to a long-ignored "divide between success at the K–12 level and the expectations of universities" (Cavanagh, 2003, p. 6).

Our failure here explains the fact that after 12 years of "English," a third or more of college students need remedial English. In the California State University system, that number is 46 percent (Harrington-

Lueker, 2002). Surely these findings help explain why about half of the students who enter college don't return for their sophomore year (Olson, 2005). The startling state of literacy education explains Graff's (2003) estimate that only 20 percent of students arrive at college with the ability to write even nominally well. Barzun observes that the typical professor is "still trying in graduate school to get decent writing and intelligent reading out of his bright students" (1991, p. 4).

Of course we expect writing to be taught in English classes—but not only there. Richard Paul points to the writing–learning connection in every discipline when he writes that "Only when students can articulate in writing the basic principles they are learning . . . can we be sure that they are internalizing those principles in an intellectually coherent way" (in Sparks, 2005, xvii). But, alas, fully 75 percent of students report that they don't do any writing in history or social studies courses (ASCD SmartBrief, 2003). Historian Sheldon Stern found that most U.S. high school students graduate having never written a single extended history paper (Fitzhugh, 2002).

The Best Is Mediocre

A special study for the National Assessment of Educational Progress asked schools to submit their students' best papers, and discovered that even the "best is mediocre" (Olson, 1995, p. 5). The highest scores came in 8th grade, where only 4 percent of students' best papers received a "high" rating. Perhaps worse yet, 43 percent of the 8th grade papers received a "low" rating.

The study also made another unexpected and important discovery: that persuasive—argumentative—writing, which cultivates students' critical reasoning capacities and prepares students for the intellectual demands of college, civic life, and the workplace, is sorely neglected. In fact, "so few examples of persuasive writing were submitted" that NAEP researchers couldn't even analyze the samples usefully (Olson, 1995, p. 5). I remember Sean Connors, the successful high school teacher mentioned in Chapter 1, cajoling his students into admitting that they had done very little writing over the years and that what they had done was seldom written in the expository, much less the persuasive, mode.

Again, it's not just poor kids or students with low grades who lack this experience. More recent NAEP studies found that even the most selective colleges and universities found poor writing among students who "all have 3.8 GPAs . . . who should be the cream of the crop." Despite the students' good grades and scores in the 1300s on their SATs, these institutions nonetheless find that the students "can't write" (Cavanagh, 2003, p. 6).

College Board officials are listening. Their advice: far more writing and rewriting, and more feedback and self-assessment as students move from drafts to final copies. In other words, it's not enough to "assign" writing; we must teach it.

Assigning Writing vs. *Teaching* Writing

For all its unparalleled cognitive benefits, "little or no real writing instruction takes place in regular classrooms" (Kameenui & Carnine, 1998, p. 72). Of the little that does occur, much of it is ineffective (p. 73).

I don't know that this is a recent development. I do know, from observing classrooms and student work, that we often "assign" writing instead of teaching it—with a cursory, often ambiguous set of instructions. Very few students receive careful, explicit instruction on how to improve a single element or feature of good writing—for instance, how to craft arresting introductory paragraphs, how to write more effective sentences, or how to effectively select and integrate quotes or supporting evidence. Most are never given multiple carefully sequenced opportunities to practice these individual elements, to receive feedback, and to study good examples that make these elements clear. As Stephanie Harvey writes, "In American education, we have traditionally asked students to write without showing them how . . . we've rarely taught the craft of writing" (1998, p. 53).

Donald Graves, whose place in the pantheon of writing researchers is secure, admits, "At one point, I realized I didn't teach; I just corrected" (Jones, 1995, p. 23). George Hillocks's pioneering meta-analytic studies found that teachers spent an average of *only three minutes explaining an assignment* before cutting kids loose to write (1987).

Writing has to be carefully taught because it is not a natural act. As Vygotsky noted, only serious training will enable most students to employ what he calls the "technology" of writing. "Such training," he points out, "requires an enormous amount of attention and effort . . . this situation recalls the development of a technical skill like piano playing (as cited in Walshe, 1987, p. 23).

A brief, general overview of the state rubric won't cut it. The most essential features of good writing—such as "word choice," or "voice" and their sub-elements—can be mastered only through repeated exposure to very focused lessons and practice opportunities that include the use of modeling and exemplars. The dramatic writing-improvement stories I have learned of and written about were a result of lessons that included continuous explanation, examples, practice, and feedback (Schmoker, 2001b). This feedback includes "self-feedback," if you will, as students were *taught,* carefully and explicitly, how to use rubrics to evaluate their own work (Stiggins, 1999, 2001).

In writing, as in reading, such well-known practices point toward enormous and predictable improvements in literacy. Among those researchers who have helped me to see this most clearly, Richard Allington is perhaps the most compelling.

The Ratio of Reading and Writing to "Stuff"

Richard Allington has emerged as one of the most trenchant but respected critics of literacy education. He has given us a useful expression that beautifully captures the startling state of English and language arts: the "reading and writing vs. 'stuff' ratio."

Allington and his teams of researchers found that only a small fraction of the time devoted to "reading" or "language arts" is spent reading or writing; most is spent on "stuff." They found that children "still spent inordinate amounts of time on workbook activities" despite the "extensive research" on the damage that results from this practice (2001, p. 27).

One culprit is the commercial reading series upon which millions of teachers depend. Used selectively, these books can be a legitimate resource, but too often they become the curriculum as they "fill up vast amounts of time with activities other than actual reading" (p. 37). Allington notes that one literature series has a ratio of 30/270 minutes of reading to other activities. (Note the rough parallel with

Calkins's 10/150 minute ratio of actual reading to "reading instruction" cited earlier.)

The problem isn't only with basal readers. Allington points to the common but counterproductive practice of accompanying a single novel with weeks of nonliterary activities. Thus, we

> Dramatically limit the volume of in-school reading . . . when we plan to spend six weeks on *Island of the Blue Dolphins,* we plan to limit children's reading. (p. 36)

And we stunt their intellectual development.

How important is this finding? Even 15 extra minutes of reading per day can lead to three months of additional growth—enough for a considerable amount of students to catch up or exceed grade-level expectations (especially if the reading is purposeful and accompanied by judicious inclusion of vocabulary development; see Marzano, 2004).

Put differently, if 90 minutes per day is devoted to reading or language arts, a 4th grader who reads *very slowly*—at the 2nd grade level—could be reading a novel like *Stone Fox* every week (Allington, 2001, p. 37). That would leave 40 minutes per day for writing, discussion, or vocabulary work—far more if some of this work were integrated into social studies, science, and beyond.

Or, as Kati Haycock has calculated: *three to four weeks* of effective, full-day literacy instruction would allow the average student to gain *an entire year* of academic growth (2005).

The Miracle of *In-School* Reading and Writing

Allington has found that as early as 1st grade, the highest-achieving classrooms spend as much as 70 percent of class time reading or responding to what they read (2001, p. 25). The benefits of time spent on purposeful reading and writing are so crucial that Allington recommends that we establish flexible standards: about 60 minutes per day of reading and 40 minutes per day of writing. Here is an idea whose time has come. New York has set a standard for the number of books each student should read—25 books per year across all subject areas (2001, p. 29). Georgia is phasing in its new standard for the same number of books, 25 per year across all subjects in grades 6 through 12.

I'm not saying students shouldn't read at home. But the value of doing an about-face from "stuff" to *in-class* reading, writing, and discussion can't be overstated. I've said enough about the underappreciated impact this would have on even our brightest and most advantaged students. But surely we can see the logic in giving disadvantaged students—who are less apt to read at home or on their own—record amounts of time to read and write during the school day. Do the math: for kids who don't or won't read at home, even an additional 30 minutes of close, purposeful reading followed by regular discussion and writing adds months of growth for each school year.

This approach is radical, but eminently realistic. Actual, existing classrooms—the best we know of—use time in this fashion. It is the most sensible, effective thing we can do if we sincerely wish to rescue kids from the time-wasting, soul-killing traditions that now deprive them of ever becoming literate—or, more precisely, *thoughtfully* literate. It would largely mean converting current amounts of time and hard work from unproductive "stuff" to literacy activities that would be far more meaningful to both students and teachers.

Arrested Development: Thoughtful Literacy vs. the 3rd Grade Slump

We've seen how research points to an opportunity for dramatic improvements in early-grade literacy. But early grade success—the ability to decode and read fluently—isn't enough. The limitations become evident in what is often referred to as the "3rd grade slump" (or 4th grade slump).

This slump happens because, from 3rd grade up, items on achievement tests, however imperfect, are predominantly inferential (Liben & Liben, 2005). Our failure to help students to read for inference and interpretation shows up big, despite the fact, as Allington points out, that

> The items attempting to assess higher-order proficiencies do not require rocket-scientist type performances. Many, in fact, require little more than the sorts of judgments about information, ideas, and assertions that an adult might need to make nearly every day. (2001, p. 8)

Instead of disparaging these tests, we need to begin teaching students the most worthy reading skills—those that require judgments about information, ideas, and assertions. We can begin this work, as Allington points out, by asking *primary-grade* students questions like the one mentioned in Chapter 6, "Who would make a better friend: Spider or Turtle?" (when reading "Hungry Spider and the Turtle").

Unfortunately, decades of research reveal our failure to build reading—or writing—instruction around such simple "higher-order thinking skills and strategies" (Allington, 2001, p. 8). We talk a lot about "active reading," but we fail to help our students to move from "decoding to strategic reading" (Vacca, 2002). Elmore found that even in schools where classrooms are orderly and students are attentive, and where reading scores have gone up, scores reach a plateau. Why? Because, as Allington points out, the reading and writing activities lack an emphasis on "interpretation, argument, and analysis" (2001, p. 27).

This all-important transition to "thoughtful literacy" can be acquired only if we teach these skills explicitly and routinely. Here, too, are some brutal facts: Allington found precious few teachers "modeling and demonstrating useful reading strategies." He observed that "most teachers offered little useful instruction" in how to read for meaning (2001, p. 31). Imagine the impact on all kids, on the achievement gap, if we began to provide daily, extended opportunities for them to read for meaning—starting in the earliest grades.

I'd love to see state assessments that more directly assess strategic reading—especially by having students put their perceptions and interpretations in written form. But the immediate problem here is not our cost-efficient (and therefore imperfect) tests. It is our decades-long failure to insist on deep, daily interpretive reading and monitor how much students engage in this type of learning. When students were asked to demonstrate their critical reading skills—in writing—they "demonstrated difficulty in providing details *and arguments* to support interpretations of what they read" (Allington, 2001, p. 27) (emphasis added).[1]

The Dullness of In-School Discussions

We see these same patterns lived out with respect to class discussions. Earlier we saw how Rose, Meier, Postman, Allington, and others found text-based intellectual exchange crucial to literacy and critical reasoning. But the Learning 24/7 study found it to be among the least common classroom activities. They observed such discussion in only 0.5 percent of classrooms (Learning 24/7, 2005). Elmore found that even these rare discussions consisted almost entirely of low-level questions (2005). Allington similarly found that in-school discussions were limp and uninteresting, nothing at all like the stimulating discussions that ordinary people have outside of school about texts they've read. He reflects on the odd anomaly that

> When you consider the richness of the talk about texts that occurs outside of schools, the typical patterns of school talk about text seem shallow and barren. (2001, p. 89)

The few discussions that do take place in schools operate on what Allington calls a "recitation script." He notes that "known-answer questions" have dominated reading lessons for as long as researchers have been closely observing classrooms. Such questions are unique to schools. They are, he chides us, "not legal in out-of-school conversations" (2001, p. 88).

Wasting Time, Wasting Lives

If we sincerely desire better schools, then our use of time must match our priorities. But as things stand, Allington writes of how

> our findings have been replicated by virtually every other research team conducting classroom-based research—we are typically distressed by how time . . . is so very inefficiently organized . . . we can readily locate another 30 to 50 minutes every day for reading and writing activity. (2001, p. 35)

I have watched, heartbroken, as a teacher of low-performing students consumed 40 minutes of a 60-minute reading period, every day, having students sing the same dozen or more songs, slowly taking attendance orally (a one-minute job turned into five, while students had to sit at rigid attention), and then doing a drawn-out, time-killing "show and tell." He almost never assessed daily instruction. School officials knowingly tolerated these practices and gave the teacher positive evaluations, year after year. Roland Barth's earlier remark about the need for "outrage at ineffective practices" comes to mind.

The brutal facts about literacy education described in this chapter are the stuff by which students' life chances are destroyed, by which the teaching profession is tarnished, by which we widen the socioeconomic divisions among our people. By winking at such malpractice, we perpetuate hopelessness and the myth that societal factors chiefly account for differences in levels of learning.

So how do we begin to make needed changes to instruction and its quality? If we're smart, we'll avail ourselves of a proven, established, and highly rewarding set of professional practices and structures. There are compelling reasons to believe that these practices are the surest, fastest route to immensely better schools. This approach is often seen in environments called "professional learning communities."

Note

1. With all the criticism directed at state assessments for being too difficult, we might consider the fact that for students from even nominally advantaged settings, they are too easy. I have seen large majorities of students pass the reading and writing sections of these tests easily—even where instruction in critical literacy has been manifestly poor or altogether missing. It is time that schools look harder at state assessment results in the "exceeds" category, which is a better indicator of authentic literacy and is an area where far fewer students make the grade.

Section III

Learning and Leading in the Professional Learning Community

Organizations only improve "where the truth is told and the brutal facts confronted."

—Jim Collins

The chapters in this section contain three arguments:

In Chapter 8, that "professional learning communities" (by whatever name), *if rightly defined,* feature the most powerful set of structures and practices for improving instruction (see Appendix B, with noted signatories supporting this claim).

In Chapter 9, I will advocate, therefore, that the most powerful actions that leaders can take are those built around the fundamental concepts of learning communities. Leadership built on this foundation will not only be simpler, but will allow ordinary leaders to have an extraordinary impact on instruction and its improvement.

In Chapter 10, I will argue that we could create the schools we've dreamed of on a grand scale—but only if we learn to embrace 1) the brutal facts about the current state of school leadership, and 2) clarity and simplicity. We need to coordinate and reinforce the few simple actions and emphases that will have profound benefits at all levels—for states, districts, schools, classrooms, and students.

8

Professional Learning Communities

The Surest, Fastest Path to Instructional Improvement

> A successful face-to-face team is more than just collectively intelligent. It makes everyone work harder, think smarter and reach better conclusions than they would have on their own.
>
> —James Surowiecki

*Teachers from Havasupai Elementary School were returning from yet another much-hyped but time-wasting workshop. In the van driving home, they began to construct, on a yellow pad, a new reading program. It was largely based on **what they already knew** but hadn't had a chance to organize or refine—the need to greatly increase time spent on meaningful reading and writing activities. Grade-level teams, with support from the principal, began to collaborate regularly and to conduct frequent common assessments, which helped them to see the impact of their efforts, by grade level, and to make adjustments to instruction. That year there were significant, and in some grades dramatic, gains in reading. The principal, seeing the results, wondered aloud why they hadn't always done business this way.*

We've seen how various forces have prevented instruction from being all it can be. And so, in these propitious times, what are the most practical, effective actions and arrangements for ensuring that instruction improves, meaningfully and steadily, in every discipline?

It may seem risky to claim that there is any "best" way to do anything. Nonetheless, a stunning number of researchers agree with Milbrey McLaughlin when she confidently asserts that

> The most promising strategy for sustained, substantive school improvement is developing the ability for school personnel to function as professional learning communities. (in DuFour & Eaker, 1998, p. xi)

Professional learning communities have emerged as arguably the best, most agreed-upon means by which to continuously improve instruction and student performance. For reasons that will become clear, they succeed where typical staff development and workshops fail.

The concurrence of the research community on this approach is quite remarkable (see the collective statement in Appendix B). More stunning yet is how rare such learning communities are in our schools and districts. Although this concept is now embraced in virtually every other industry and profession, we are way behind in instituting it in schools (Wise, 2004; Wagner, 2004).

Learning Communities: Fundamental Concepts

But what are true "learning communities," and why are they more effective than traditional staff development? Whether we call them "communities of practice" or "self-managing teams," clarity is crucial. If we are sloppy here, failure will follow. We can't afford, as Rick DuFour points out, to corrupt or co-opt the "fundamental concepts" of collaborative learning communities (2004). What are those fundamental concepts?

First, professional learning communities require that teachers establish a common, concise set of essential curricular standards and teach to them on a roughly common schedule. Teams need to consult their state assessment guides and other documents to help them make wise decisions about what to teach (and what not to teach).

Then they must meet regularly. I suggest that teams meet at least twice a month, for a minimum of 45 minutes, to help one another teach to these selected standards (I have seen great things come of

30-minute meetings). This time must be very focused; most of it must be spent talking in "concrete, precise terms" about instruction with a concentration on "thoughtful, explicit examination of practices *and their consequences*"—the results achieved with specific lessons and units (Little, 1990, p. 519). Or, as Bob Eaker asks, "Based on a collaborative analysis of the results of our efforts, what can we do to improve student learning?" (2002, p. 21). To perform this work, teachers must make frequent use of common assessments. These assessments (the use of which Doug Reeves refers to as the "gold standard" of true assessment literacy), are pivotal. With common assessments and results, teachers can conduct what Eaker calls "active research" where "a culture of experimentation prevails" (2002, p. 21).

These simple, fundamental concepts combine a "guaranteed and viable curriculum" (Marzano, 2003) with continual analysis of actual lessons and units, and improvement of instruction. These elements, so rarely emphasized in school or state improvement or accreditation plans, deserve our attention *more than anything else we do in the name of school improvement* (Schmoker, 2002). Failed attempts to establish professional learning communities can usually be traced to a lack of fidelity to these fundamental concepts.

Many educators are starting to define the ideal professional learning community as the entire school or district—including the state department. As we'll see in the next chapter, this is an excellent development, as long as we don't lose sight of the central importance of small, instructionally focused teacher teams as the basic unit of professional learning communities. Indeed, schools will be much more successful when entire districts and state departments emphatically reinforce and support teacher teamwork and operate using the same empirical processes: the same team-based, short-term implementation, assessment, and adjustment cycle that effective teaching teams employ.

Getting Teamwork Wrong

Unfortunately, most so-called "teamwork" lacks these essential features. There are dangers here. Decades ago, Judith Little found that most team talk floats high above the level of implementation: "distant from the real work in and of the classroom" (1987, p. 507). Instead of closely and constructively examining practice, most teams serve to "confirm present practice without evaluating its worth"—in other words, without using short-term assessment results as the basis for improvement (1990, p. 517).

Almost 20 years later, the situation hasn't changed. Little and her colleagues found that teams continue to discuss "wide-ranging issues" instead of looking closely and analytically at teaching, and at *how their teaching affects learning* on an ongoing basis. They found that the traditional ethos of the buffer—"non-interference, privacy, and harmony"—still prevails at the expense of improved instruction (Little et al., 2003).

We have to be very clear about what true teamwork entails: a regular schedule of formal meetings where teachers focus on the details of their lessons and adjust them on the basis of assessment results. The use of common assessments is essential here. Without these, teams can't discern or enjoy the impact of their efforts on an ongoing basis. Enjoying and celebrating these short-term results is the very key to progress, to achieving "momentum" toward improvement (Collins, 2001a).

There are deeply practical reasons that team-based "learning communities" have become, in both education and industry, the state of the art for improving performance. As Tom Peters has written, self-managing teams have become "the basic organizational building block" in effective companies (1987, p. 297). Let's look at the reasons why.

Why Professional Learning Communities? Why Now?

We have relied far too much, with miserable results, on a failed model for improving instructional practice: training, in the form of workshops or staff development. Despite the millions of teacher-hours we've invested in such training, it has, by common consent, been monumentally ineffective (Corcoran, Fuhrman, & Belcher, 2001; Guskey, 2003; Sparks, 2001a). In fact, Dennis Sparks, the executive director of the National Staff Development Council (NSDC) urges schools to see that professional learning communities are indeed the best form of staff development (Sparks, 1998). We saw in Chapter 1 that the NSDC ran a series of blunt ads in *Phi Delta Kappan* (2004) decrying the ineffectiveness of most professional development (Sparks, 1998).

What's missing? For one thing, professional development often is bad beyond hope. Second, most of it typically makes no formal, immediate arrangements for teachers to translate learning into actual lessons or units, whose impact we assess and then use as the basis for ongoing improvement. Without this simple cycle, training is irrelevant. Finally, training characteristically promotes a mentality of dependence. Training implies that teachers must depend on new or external guidance because they don't know enough about instruction to begin making serious improvements. But teachers do have this capability—if, that is, they pool their practical knowledge by working in teams.

True learning communities work against such dependency. Unlike typical staff development, learning communities encourage teachers to recognize and share the best of what they already know. This approach insists on the fundamental elements that workshops routinely ignore: collective follow-up, assessment, and adjustment of instruction. In a five-year period during which Adlai Stevenson High School made immense achievement gains, not a single external staff development initiative was launched. Their gains were the result of internal expertise, shared and refined by groups of teachers.

Effective team-based learning communities—not workshops—are the very best kind of professional development. Other countries learned this long ago.

Lesson Study: Team-Based Continuous Improvement

In Japan and Germany, they don't do professional development on the American model. Instead, school leaders arrange for teams of teachers to meet regularly to create—to craft and refine—lessons and teaching units until they have the maximum impact on student learning (Stigler & Hiebert, 1999). The teacher teams carefully deliberate over each step and the best possible sequence of steps in the lesson; how to most effectively introduce and explain the concept; how much time to devote to practice exercises; and how to assess and adjust *during and after* each lesson and unit.

When a lesson works well, educators publish it (in books you can buy in convenience stores). Practitioners provide demonstration lessons for other teachers at "lesson fairs." These fairs represent professional development at its best—conducted by professionals themselves.

If we think that training or "pro-dev" typically leads to such carefully crafted lessons, we are mistaken. This is the chief reason staff development has little or no impact on practice—or on learning results.

This simple approach may seem unexciting to some; there is no big send-off, no program launch—just regular team meetings, year after year, where teachers help one another find a better lesson for teaching subtraction with regrouping, or effective introductions to persuasive essays, for example.

Collins points out that the most powerful improvement actions will "appear boring and pedestrian" to those who love glitzy initiatives and programs (2001a, p. 142). We have to see how this seemingly mundane concern with creating, testing, and refining lessons and units, in teams, is the real—guaranteed—path to better instruction. Our resistance to such procedures represents no less than a battle over the soul of school improvement.

Teams vs. Workshops

A team of 5th grade teachers at Holaway Elementary School saw steady, considerable improvements at each consecutive team meeting. They learned, by analyzing their common assessment results, that their math rubric needed to be much more carefully taught (not just quickly explained), point by point, with examples and opportunities to practice and receive feedback; they learned that self-assessment also needed to be taught, and they learned from one another how to teach it, carefully and explicitly, so that students became less dependent on the teacher for their learning. And teachers learned to depend on their colleagues instead of outside experts.

Such results can be achieved anywhere, wherever people have learned that collective effort and intelligence are the most powerful force for improvement—more powerful than "even the most knowledgeable individuals working alone" (Little, 1990, p. 520). As Surowiecki discovered, teams are almost always "genuinely smarter than the smartest people within them" (2004, p. 182). Because of this, we must re-evaluate our workshops and standard-issue staff development, which have had such a miserable payoff. Workshops "do not work," Stiggins points out, because they "don't permit the application and experimentation in real classrooms, and sharing that experience in a team effort" (1999, p. 198). Teamwork, not training, fosters continuous, targeted attention to the details and the impact of effective lessons and units.

If we are going to conduct workshops, let's insist on a radically different format: they should be designed on this same team-based, cyclical format that focuses immediately on producing lessons and then evaluating and refining them on the basis of results. If we're smart, we'll pilot workshops with only a single team (instead of an entire school or district) until the team produces a convincing body of short-term assessment results. In the main, let's have our own teams provide professional development, by sharing their most successful lessons and units at "lesson fairs"—always with their assessment results (Stigler & Hiebert, 1999). Organized teamwork combined with such lesson fairs perfectly captures what is meant by a true "professional learning community."

Fortunately, more educators are becoming at least familiar with "lesson study." But it concerns me that many teachers still write it off as an exotic, time-consuming process that we can't imitate or adapt. That is a misconception.

Making Lesson Study Our Own: The 20-Minute Team Meeting

In my workshops, I like to do a pared-down version of lesson study. I take teachers through an entire team meeting—from identifying a low-scoring standard, to roughing out an appropriate assessment, to

building a lesson designed to help as many students as possible succeed on the assessment. We do all this—somewhat crudely—in less
than 20 minutes. Once completed, we take a break, and then we posit
that the lesson didn't work as well as we'd like. So we make a revision
or two.

The results can be surprising: teachers see that in even so short
a time, they can collectively craft fairly coherent, effective standards-
based lessons and assessments. Many also realize that such careful
lesson planning, matched with a carefully built assessment, is new
terrain—much different than simply "assigning" an exercise or activity
from a textbook. Lights go on: they realize that learning to make such
focused, constructive effort virtually *requires* teamwork, that the members not only contribute a richer pool of ideas but—hugely important—
social commitment and energy, an essential element of success (Fullan, 1991, p. 84). They realize that careful, collective planning is bound
to result in lessons that will produce far better assessment results.

The importance of these factors helps to explain, as we saw in
Chapter 1, why 72 percent of students in one class succeed on an
assessment, while right next door only 26 percent succeed (Marzano,
2003, p. 7). *God is in the details.*

Ideally, about twice as much time should be devoted to such
team meetings—more if you have it. Whether we are talking about
short or long meetings, most teachers admit that they have seldom, or
never, met to create a detailed lesson or unit with colleagues in their
entire professional lives. Fewer still have ever reconvened to look at
the results and enjoy their success or make adjustments to the lesson.
Most realize how such routines could have a seismic impact on learning levels. They also realize that they know more than enough about
teaching to get started at such work *immediately, in most cases without
any additional training.* It is time to use what we know. I have worked
with teams, who, within a meeting or two, were able to produce lessons that enabled almost 100 percent of their students to master standards where the majority had previously failed. For example, they
focused on effective introductions to essays, operations with positive
and negative integers, or descriptive settings.

Not every lesson needs to be created by the team. But such interaction illustrates how regular opportunities to help one another construct, assess, and refine lessons, units, and assessments could have an impact far beyond each team-made lesson or unit. If teachers met even every other week for such work, it would reinforce the value and the "craft" of creating effective lessons that contain the essential elements so often neglected.

And something else: in an environment that focuses on a leaner, more potent set of "power standards," teachers and entire systems would quickly begin to build up a rich, adaptable repertoire of effective lessons and assessments, which could in turn be shared and showcased on designated occasions (if "staff development days" became "lesson fairs"). At Adlai Stevenson and in other districts, teacher teams have organized a wealth of great standards-based lessons that teachers—new or veteran—can consult for years to come.

I wish I had worked in such a school; I wish all my daughters' teachers could work in such a productive, professional environment.

Why Professional Learning Communities? Teachers Tell Us Why

I like to finish this team activity by asking participants to discuss the reasons so many scholars, professors, and researchers from education and industry agree that such structured, team-based effort is perhaps the most effective way to improve performance in any enterprise. Having just experienced a successful team meeting, teachers can point to the manifold and distinctive benefits—for novices and veterans alike. They find the meetings

- Ensure follow-up and reflection on instruction and its impact.

- Are results-oriented. The assessment piece (so often left out) becomes the basis for further adjustment or improvement.

- Reinforce a focus on essential common standards aligned with state assessments, providing a guaranteed and viable curriculum.

- Are *social.* They create the best kind of accountability—which relies on our commitment to people we know and care about, our colleagues and students. (As DuFour points out, *loyalty runs strongest* at the smallest unit—the team—where people work together to achieve common goals.)

- Honor and empower teachers and their intelligence, capturing the vast reserves of expertise in any team and school.

As we can see, there is a rich rationale for establishing these structures in all schools, without delay.

The Experts Are Among Us

One of the reasons such teamwork and lesson study are so effective is that they tap into teachers' existing capabilities and potential, which are more apt to flourish in teams than under external trainers.

An army of staff developers currently consumes precious time that should be spent creating, assessing, and refining lessons and units in teams. It is safe to say that the preponderance of staff development—let's not mince words—never asks teachers to do such things.

Dennis Sparks, who deeply understands effective staff development, put it starkly for me once: he said that any faculty could begin improving performance, tomorrow morning, if they never attended another workshop in their lives. They would improve, inexorably, simply by deciding on what they wanted students to learn and then working together to prepare, test, and refine lessons and strategies—continuously, toward better results.

We are still too tentative here. We act as though viable improvement must be acquired from certified experts in a series of presentations, with PowerPoint slide shows and projectors.

Our never-sated quest for the right program or training reinforces the notion that teachers need more information or more training or the "right" program before they can proceed confidently toward improvement. We have created what Fullan and Hargreaves call a "culture of dependency" that disempowers teachers and is a barrier to smart, constructive effort (1996, p. 24).

Let's peek behind the curtain here. For those of us perennially addicted to the next new training, Jim Block has this to say: "we have all the skills, the tools, the training that we need" (in Sparks, 2003b, p. 52).

I worked with members of a high school English department who had known one another for years. They made an interesting discovery—that when they finally began to pick each other's brains on how to most effectively teach a clear, specific standard, something magical happened—even (or especially) in focused, 40-minute meetings. They began to share and refine the collective wealth of *what they already knew*. They found that they could create lessons that allowed record numbers of students to master the most sophisticated writing skills, one lesson at a time, at their poor, high-minority high school.

I've worked with brand-new teachers whose untapped fund of expertise emerged only in the focused, socially charged context of a good team meeting—not unlike what we see in television shows like "CSI"—where brainstorming leads to major practical breakthroughs in mere minutes (I'm a big fan of brainstorming). Often enough, even these breakthroughs are merely reminders or refinements of strategies that are widely known, but half-forgotten, or commonsense variations and extensions of those practices.

Acting on What We Know: The "Knowing-Doing Gap"

Teachers know a lot about good practice. But school systems, ever-seduced by the next new thing, don't provide them with focused, collaborative opportunities that remind and reinforce the implementation of the most basic and powerful practices.

Is it accurate to assume the following?

• The majority of teachers know that students need to do lots of purposeful reading and writing.

• The script of a lesson or unit must include a clear explanation of the specific standard.

• Modeling and step-by-step demonstration of new skills is essential.

- Short practice opportunities combined with a "check for understanding" ensure that more kids learn and fewer are left behind.

Teachers know that a good lesson includes an assessment that aligns with the standards just taught. Most teachers have learned a few strategies for keeping kids attentive—for example, calling on kids randomly, not on those who always raise their hands. Most have learned (thanks to decades of work by people like Richard Stiggins, Grant Wiggins, and Jay McTighe) that we should frequently provide exemplars of good work and that we need to be very clear about our grading and evaluative criteria if we want them to succeed. Classroom studies continue to reveal that these basic, powerful practices are still all too rare.

But instead of making arrangements for teachers to more consistently implement and refine these well-known, high-leverage strategies, we adopt programs or plans or attend workshops that have almost no effect on the fundamental practices listed above.

We can't claim ignorance here. I'm not saying that every teacher understands or can execute these elements perfectly, but most have learned them in undergraduate preparation or elsewhere. Almost any team of teachers knows enough, collectively, to get started on adapting and refining them, with increasing success. But teachers can't—or won't—until we stop interrupting this work with yet another strategic plan or book study or series of workshops that prevents them from spending time focusing collectively, and at long last, on more effective lessons. As Block warns us, we have to resist the "default mechanism that directs us to *study and learn more* rather than to *take action using what we already know*" (in Sparks, 2003b, p. 53) (emphasis added).

Just do it. As Pfeffer and Sutton point out, the most powerful, high-leverage practices are indeed rare, but seldom difficult or complex. The most vital, concrete improvements

> are far from rocket science. They are, in fact, common sense . . .
> successful interventions rely more on *implementation of simple
> knowledge* than on creating new insights or discovering obscure or
> secret practices. (2000, pp. 14–15) (emphasis added)

Implementing what we already know points, once again, to the need for structured collaboration and experimentation. Even "research-based practices" are like raw material: of very limited value until they are intelligently integrated in context.

Knowledge Isn't Steel

Pfeffer and Sutton describe how the least-effective organizations "treat knowledge pretty much like steel or any other resource, to be gathered, shared, and distributed" (2000, p. 18). But knowledge—like research-based teaching practices—is only as good as its intelligent application.

I routinely ask audiences if they know or have read Marzano's highly useful book *Classroom Instruction That Works* (Marzano, Pickering, & Pollock, 2001). Almost everyone has. Many have been involved in a book study or attended several workshops on the use of these methods. But when I ask how many have implemented them, if anyone has monitored or even asked about how the strategies were used and with what effect on specific assessment results, the room grows very quiet.

"Identifying similarities and differences" is a powerful teaching strategy—at the top of Marzano's list. But it won't have much impact until a team finds a good situation in which to apply it, until we adapt and adjust this strategy on the basis of assessment results in actual lessons.

Knowledge isn't steel. As Richard Allington has pointed out, even the best research is "a slippery beast" (2001, p. 9), of no value whatever until we experiment with it, until we find the right way to integrate it into a lesson that gets great assessment results. Best practices don't pay off until they have been implemented and fine-tuned in short-term, closely studied cycles. Such empirical efforts need to become the norm, the stuff of a new, more professional "culture of experimentation" in teaching (Eaker, 2002, p. 21).

A New Culture of Teaching

Unfortunately, few teachers see themselves as inventive, adaptive professionals upon whom improvement primarily depends. Fullan is emphatic here, decrying the "dependency" of teachers whose "intellectual and investigative effectiveness" we have failed to culti-vate—or believe in (in Sparks, 2003a, p. 56). For Hiebert and Stigler, professionalism itself is at stake:

> When teachers recognize that knowledge for improvement is something they can generate, rather than something that must be handed to them by so-called experts, they are on a new profes-sional trajectory. They are on the way to building a true profession of teaching, a profession in which members take responsibility for steady and lasting improvement. They are building a new culture of teaching. (2004, p. 15)

This new professional trajectory starts with a recognition that we must identify and cultivate the talent that already resides within our schools.

Recognizing Our "Positive Deviants"

The evidence continues to mount that internal expertise is of more value than what we import. Instruction improves when teachers, in teams, *teach each other* the practice of teaching" (Little, 1990, p. 509). As Rosenholtz found, teachers learn best not from outsiders but from one another (1991).

Anthony Alvarado was superintendent of New York City's District 2 for several years, during which time he worked with Richard Elmore and Milbrey McLaughlin (whose research on professional learning communities is seminal). One of Alvarado's chief improvement strate-gies was to look within: he identified the district's best teachers and provided organized opportunities for teachers to learn from them and from one another. Interestingly, the greatest opportunities—and gains—came from a focus on greatly increasing the amount of authen-tic reading and writing in all classes (Bradley, 1993). During Alvarado's tenure, District 2 rose from 16th to 2nd among New York City's 32 school districts (New York City Leadership Academy, 2003).

Jerry Sternin, formerly of Harvard Business School, spent years working on seemingly "unsolvable" problems—such as malnutrition in Vietnam. His research team, on the verge of abandoning its effort, discovered that certain groups and families—"positive deviants"—had found simple, replicable solutions to this problem. The team visited these families and then had tremendous success replicating their practices in the wider community after attempts to impose outside solutions had failed.

The team's approach worked because "internal expertise" was more trusted within the community: it provoked less resistance and needed less fine-tuning. The very same strategy that would be rejected if it came from an outsider was embraced and replicated if it came from within. Like Pfeffer and Sutton, Block, and others, the team found that the solutions simply aren't "out there," Sternin notes. "You can't bring permanent solutions in from the outside" (in Sparks, 2004, p. 48).

Best of all, it turns out that every organization has such "positive deviants," whose accomplishments are routinely overlooked. Kati Haycock notes that "virtually every high poverty school has some spectacularly wonderful teachers" (2005).

If these teachers and teams are identified (the job of the school and district), their success and expertise can lead to expanded success and can inspire, as no outsider can, a vision of what's possible. Because these spectacular teachers are local, they are your most credible and effective trainers. And unlike trainers from out of town, they are available when it counts: after the session, when teachers encounter problems and need clarity and encouragement.

Winning Teams and the Magic of Momentum

In *Good to Great,* Collins shares the same discovery: that external solutions wreak havoc on the culture of improvement (2001a). Effective organizations overcome resistance with results generated by people within their own company. They ceaselessly share and point to these accomplishments so that people realize that they too can become "members of a winning team." When they see evidence of success, they "are likely to say 'That'll work. Count me in'" (p. 177). This recognition leads to yet more home-grown action that leads in turn to more results, to more "tangible evidence" that continues to build confidence and capacity and "the magic of momentum" (2001b; p. 98).

The process begins when we present evidence of in-school or in-district success. Any school or district can jump-start its improvement effort by reviewing its own data. This review will reveal a surprising number of "positive deviants," teachers and teams who now perform quietly but exceptionally. These people—make no mistake—are literally closing the achievement gap, sometimes considerably. Best of all, as Haycock (and I and many others) have found, every school and district has them. We need to learn to share this information sensitively, explaining its importance as we go. And we can't continue to hide exceptional performance to avoid making others uncomfortable; the stakes are too high.

We've seen how Sean Connors's very replicable teaching methods resulted in tremendous gains—26 percent in one year in his high-poverty high school. But, as in most school systems, he was never given the chance to amplify his influence. We've seen how an 8th grade team in Arizona achieved the highest writing scores in the state by using strategies that were equally replicable. They were given the chance to share their strategies and results, which inspired other successful efforts. In the Brazosport Independent School District in Texas, one of the catalysts for improvement was the "tangible results" achieved by Mary Barksdale, whose exceptional success in the district's poorest school inspired teams throughout the district to adapt and refine her methods. Her results, sensibly shared by district leadership, were the starting point for Brazosport's breathtaking turnaround—becoming both the highest-achieving and most-improved school district in the state (Schmoker, 2001b, p. 108).

The principle of positive deviance abets the central tenets of teamwork: that teachers learn best from one another, from people in their own organizations. We should, therefore, be sharing the compelling case for teamwork and engaging in dialogue as we make this transition. At some point, teamwork should be established as the new norm, just as it is in other professions (Peters, 1987; Wagner, 2004; Wise, 2004). Educators should obsessively celebrate, study, and showcase every team success, and honor successful teams by creating as many opportunities as possible for internal experts to provide—and be compensated for—internal staff development, always and only on the basis of measurable assessment results. All stunningly simple, common-sense strategies. All dismayingly, unnecessarily, rare.

Unfortunately, none of this will happen until we radically reorient the work of school improvement toward internal expertise and self-managing teams, which predominant structures now undermine.

Tipping Point: From Long-Term Plans to Lesson Plans

If we reflect on what we know about the power of internal expertise, we should realize that the major shift needed in schools is not unlike what occurred in business and industry. As we saw in Chapter 1, the elaborate, long-term machinations of managers and planners can't compare to what practitioners—working in data-driven, goal-oriented "self-managing teams"—can accomplish. A number of real schools demonstrate that when we grant these teams both autonomy and responsibility for short-term results, we will find that their on-the-ground expertise has an incalculably larger and more direct impact on instruction and achievement (Schmoker, 1999, 2001b). Virtually every enterprise has realized that people work smarter, faster, and more happily under such circumstances (Peters, 1987; Surowiecki, 2004). Goal-oriented teamwork trumps remote, large-scale strategic planning and "teacher-proof" programs any day of the week. Every tenable study has arrived at this conclusion (Mintzberg, 1994; Pfeffer & Sutton, 2000; others in Schmoker, 2004).

But for the purposes of this chapter, we should look at how complex plans thwart improvement by consuming and thus supplanting the focus, time, and energy that could be devoted to team-based learning. I've looked at hundreds of plans, and none of them—not one—clearly and emphatically arranged for teams to develop and refine lessons on the basis of results. Strategic plans, by their very nature, run in an entirely different direction from collaborative learning communities. Instead of simplicity and economy, we get needless bureaucracy, length, and complexity—which are the enemy of focus and which crowd out the time and possibility for teamwork focused on instruction.

As much as anything, these plans are hobbled by their characteristic reverence for the "long term." Unlike the best organizations, schools have yet to learn that in order to succeed, we need to gear up to achieve fast, tangible results.

The Need for Speed: Quick Wins and Effective Teamwork

The case for generating a steady stream of short-term team "wins" is not new and is pure common sense. If anything, it is mystifying that schools have yet to institute structures that allow people to see that their hard work is paying off—this week or month—not next year or five years from now. Tom Peters, Kouzes and Posner, and many others began to urge an emphasis on quick, frequent small wins in the 1980s. John Kotter (as cited in Fullan, 2001) urged us to "generate short-term wins" (p. 32). Gary Hamel exhorts us to "Win small, win early, win often" (as cited in Fullan, 2001, p. 33). For Bob Eaker, our goals themselves should be "designed to produce short-term wins" (2002, p. 17). And now Jim Collins tells us to scrap the big plans in favor of producing a "steady stream of successes," which in turn will create "the magic of momentum" toward enduring organizational success (in Schmoker, 2004, p. 427).

Here indeed is a knowing-doing gap. If we rectified it, we could have an electrifying effect on schools and those who work in them. The solution starts with teams:

• Starline Elementary School in Lake Havasu City, Arizona: the 1st grade team began celebrating gains in writing at each of their short, but very powerful monthly meetings. They had only 25 minutes—they met during lunch. Simple, hand-made bar charts helped make these gains exciting and tangible for team members.

• Peck Elementary in Arvada, Colorado: team members saw monthly gains on areas of difficulty in math and language arts well before they saw sizeable annual improvement gains on the Colorado State Assessment Program.

• Donaldson Elementary School in Tucson: a powerful lesson plan (created in about 15 minutes) resulted in 85 out of 88 students being able to write effective "descriptive settings"—up from only 4 students a month earlier.

Happily, the emphasis on such short-term wins is supported by the growing awareness that short-term formative assessment has an immense impact on learning results[1] (Black & Wiliam, 1998; Stiggins, 1999). Although we still rarely see teams implement and review short-term assessments *for* learning, the value of this approach is now widely acknowledged. Again, it is easy to see why such common, teacher-made, formative assessments constitute what Doug Reeves regards as the "gold standard" of assessment. Formative assessments not only inform productive adjustments to instruction but also ensure consistently delivered, viable curriculum as they allow teams to see, on a frequent basis, that their efforts are paying off.

A Simple Plan: Making the Transition to Professional Learning Communities

Unless we already work in organizations where teams are producing a steady stream of successful lessons, the best plan to pursue is to convert our schools and districts into true learning communities. We need to celebrate and share the results of *the very first short-term team win* that rolls in and every one thereafter, as teams and schools and districts—and whole states—realize that they can achieve ever-improved results, one lesson, one unit, one "small win" at a time.

And so it only makes sense to define—to radically redefine—leadership on the basis of team-based professional learning communities.

Note

1. For those wanting to create and integrate formative assessments, Peter Campbell, the lead instructional designer at Montclair State University, points out that most formative assessments we purchase from an external vendor have serious limitations and disadvantages. For all their ease in implementation and their capacity to promote an initial increase in scores, vendor-created assessments predominantly consist of lower-order and multiple-choice test items. And they promote, once again, the culture of "dependence" that continues to make teaching less, rather than more, professional and satisfying. This is not the direction in which we should head (Campbell, 2005).

9 Leadership in the Professional Learning Community

> No institution can survive if it needs geniuses or supermen to manage it. It must be organized to get along under a leadership of average human beings.
>
> —Peter Drucker

We know that in too many schools and classrooms, instruction is a mere shadow of what it could be, especially with respect to critical reasoning. We also know that if teachers worked in productive, instructionally focused teams, we could indeed enter that "era of unprecedented effectiveness" that Marzano and others predict. But will most school leaders, our "average human beings" in Drucker's phrase, be able to grasp this opportunity? I believe they can, but only if we radically simplify and refocus the leaders' time and duties.

My Favorite Case History

The best article I've ever read on school leadership is Richard DuFour's "The Learning-Centered Principal" (2002). In it, the former principal, then superintendent of Adlai Stevenson High School, describes how he underwent a very deep and important change. In painful detail, DuFour outlines his efforts to take the traditional supervision model as far as it could go. He kept a grueling schedule of classroom observations, pre-conferences, and post-conferences—way beyond the legal requirements. Surely, he thought, this effort would result in increased achievement.

DuFour was wrong. Odd as it may sound, he realized he was too focused on teaching, not enough on learning—on assessment results. As he puts it, he went from being an "instructional leader" to becoming a "learning leader," something very different and—of utmost importance—much more within the reach of average leaders. He began to spend far less time observing and advising teachers in the role of expert and far more time discussing and supporting learning— short-term assessment results—with his directors and teams of teachers. His time and attention were now refocused on simply monitoring and supporting success on common, formative assessments. DuFour came to the profound realization that teachers learn more from one another, working in teams, than from a single harried supervisor, running frenetically from teacher to teacher, giving advice.

But he also learned that certain conditions had to exist for teachers to learn from one another:

First, improved short-term (weekly, monthly, quarterly) and annual results were *non-negotiable*. To create a sense of urgency and goal-orientation (no easy thing in an affluent, already high-achieving setting), he collected data from comparably situated schools. The data revealed that his school's achievement levels, however high, didn't compare all that favorably with some of the best. Faculty members used this data to set measurable, time-bound improvement goals and to target specific areas of opportunity, where performance was lowest.

The next step was pivotal. For every course in their curriculum, including electives, he had teachers carefully review state and district documents and then carefully select and teach *only the most essential* standards. Strict limits were set on the number of topics and concepts that could be taught in any course. They then built their own in-district, end-of-course, formative assessments around these selected standards. These internally created assessments guaranteed a viable curriculum and were aligned with state assessments and Advanced Placement and college entrance exams.

He then created a schedule that allowed same-course teacher teams to meet two to three times a month, on a regular schedule, to prepare and improve their lessons together on the basis of results—from their common, formative assessments.

All good, but one more procedure was necessary: DuFour or one of his directors *met with teams on a regular basis* simply to ask variations on the following questions:

> To what extent were students learning the intended outcomes of each course?
>
> and
>
> What steps can I take to give both students and teachers the time and support they need to improve learning? (2002, p. 13)

I contend that any leader in any school could establish and eventually master these same reasonable, time-efficient procedures. They would lead, almost immediately, to better teaching and to ever-improving levels of achievement. I would advocate that such simple practices and conditions become the new fundamentals of leadership—and that leaders be allowed to "stop doing" (one of Collins's mantras) most of what now diverts them from these powerful, commonsense procedures (Collins, 2001a).

A Focus on Learning

Notice in this simple scheme how a focus on *learning,* on assessment results, becomes the leverage for improvements in *teaching,* which is only as good as its impact on learning. When leadership is focused on results, on urging a formal, frequent review of the impact of instruction, teaching improves. Little and her colleagues speak to this (with classic understatement) when they observe that "the impulse to talk about teaching might have been better served by sustaining closer and longer attention to the available *evidence of student learning*" (Little et al., 2003, p. 191) (emphasis added).

Through such results-oriented team efforts, Adlai Stevenson High School became a national and then world-class school—rated at one point among the top 20 schools in the world (DuFour, 1995, p. 35). For more than a decade, the school enjoyed uninterrupted achievement gains, receiving an array of national and international awards—not for flashy programs but for academic achievements.

Stevenson's rise to prominence actually speaks to two primary issues. First, that these new structures and practices are eminently reasonable, rational, and within reach of any school or leader. To succeed, we need to make this case to all parties carefully and patiently.

Second, because these structures and practices run counter to the "awful inertia" of traditional supervision, large-scale progress may require unprecedented and unified support from districts and states. Such support will greatly increase the odds that our schools will reach their tipping point, a large-scale shift to instructional and supervisory practices that will transform schooling as we know it.

Redefining Leadership: The Power of Simplicity and Economy

In a study of successful school districts, *Beyond Islands of Excellence,* the Learning First Alliance found that large-scale improvement will elude us until we redefine leadership (Togneri, 2003). How? Along the same lines we have emphasized here: cutting through layers of complacence to acknowledge our manifold opportunities for better performance, and using ongoing assessment data to keep it real and to monitor progress. And—importantly—by replacing conventional professional development with regular times for self-managing teams to prepare and improve their lessons together.

On this last point, the researchers were emphatic: these "island" school districts were successful—across socioeconomic lines— because leaders understood that effective teamwork is fundamental to success. It was important that these districts "worked on working together" (2003, p. 9).

This approach makes leadership simpler. It is radically redirected from satisfying long lists of bureaucratic requirements to simply *equipping and supporting teams* at every level to solve problems and generate the small wins that mark and promote continuous improvement.

Such simplicity may seem simplistic, but it is not. This leadership strategy is actually quite consistent with the team-focused "simplicity and diligence" and "simple plans" that Collins found to be the hallmark of effective organizations (2001a, p. 177). The most successful companies have always been distinguished by their "incredible simplicity" and "simple, simple, simple ideas" (2001a, pp. 94–95). Pfeffer and Sutton are similarly struck by the emphasis on "simplicity and common sense" in organizations that make teamwork their "core value" (2000, p. 56). Years ago, Tom Peters urged us to "stop rejecting the simple" (1987, p. 160). The best companies eliminated entire layers of management and supervision to unleash the untapped energy and expertise of "self-managing teams" (1987, p. 282).

In leadership, as with curriculum, less is more. Effective leaders, writes Collins, "see what is essential and ignore the rest" (2001a, p. 91). He urges us to "focus on what is vital—and to eliminate all of the extraneous distractions . . . stop doing the senseless things that consume so much time and energy" (2001b, p. 104). Peter Drucker similarly admonishes us to recognize that

> the easiest and the greatest increases in productivity in knowledge work come from redefining the task and especially from eliminating what need not be done. (in DuFour & Eaker, 1998, p. 151)

As Anthony Alvarado told *Education Week,* "When you have a very clear focus, you recognize what's important and all the other stuff becomes not important" (Bradley, 1993, p. 6).

That "other stuff" is killing us. A new, more powerful conception of leadership begins with the recognition that we must eliminate the senseless things that now divert leaders' time and attention away from the two elements most vital to school success: *how* we teach, which is best improved through focused teacher collaboration, and *what* we teach—in Marzano's words, "a guaranteed and viable curriculum."

Leadership Starts with a Commitment to a Guaranteed and Viable Curriculum

Marzano's meta-analytic studies formalized the colossal importance of a guaranteed and viable curriculum. But it is pure common sense that more students will learn in schools where leaders monitor what gets taught—to ensure that every student has roughly the same opportunities to read and write and to learn essential standards.

A common, high-quality curriculum is just as important to the team itself. Without it, team members lack a shared focus; they can't even work together effectively. Leaders must arrange for teacher teams to map out a common schedule for teaching the standards they themselves select to teach in each course. We've seen that this team scheduling is essential to success (Marzano, 2003; Haycock, 2005). In a moment, we'll see simple, practical ways by which both leaders and teachers can ensure that these standards *are actually taught* (the real challenge).

It doesn't matter what we call this work or its final product—a "curriculum map" or a "pacing guide." But it must reflect serious attention (not lockstep conformity) to the best state-assessed standards and to intellectual engagement—to the power standards at the upper end of Bloom's taxonomy.

At Adlai Stevenson High School, leaders call this foundational work the "Curriculum Development Process" (DuFour & Eaker, 1998, p. 166). To complete it, administrators should grant primary responsibility—leadership—to teams and departments themselves to select and map only the most essential standards to be taught in any course (it is always smart to put fairly strict, numerical limits on the number of major concepts and standards taught, by course). These maps might then be reviewed by resident experts to ensure their "viability"—their attention to only the most important learning outcomes—and their alignment with state assessments.

But these efforts aren't enough. Despite the many workshops now offered on curriculum mapping, my most recent classroom tours and teacher interviews confirm that in most cases instruction still does not match the most viable standards. We have to monitor.

The Courage to Monitor

Decades ago, Dan Lortie wrote that "the monitoring of effective instruction is the heart of effective instruction" (1975, p. 41). I believe we won't have a guaranteed and viable curriculum until principals or teacher leaders begin to meet with teacher teams by month or quarter to review and discuss evidence of what is actually being taught.

Robert Marzano recommends the same kind of administrative review (2003, p. 31), and Richard and Rebecca DuFour conducted them for years. These reviews provide an occasion for teams to demonstrate that the essential, agreed-upon learning outcomes are being taught—and how successfully—per the results on common, formative assessments. They also provide an opportunity for teams to reflect on results, discuss problems, and ask for support from the leader or administrator on a frequent, timely basis.

Does it even need to be said that there is simply no substitute for such regular reviews, focused on teaching and its impact, between teachers and leaders? In many schools, such reviews would have more impact than all the initiatives we have ever launched, combined.

But such reviews violate everything that has been so private and protected over the decades—the "don't ask, don't tell" culture, which still pretends that we provide a coherent curriculum when we clearly don't (though there are signs of modest progress). Courage and commitment are essential here because the stakes are so high: the absence of a guaranteed and viable curriculum will doom any improvement effort.

Until such reviews (or some tough-minded equivalent) become as common as school desks, there is no sense in expecting serious improvements in teaching and learning.

The Power of the Quarterly Curriculum Review

For leaders to be effective, we have to make it less difficult for them to ask for evidence that essential standards are being taught, for evidence of how many students are learning those standards. The following forms of evidence would facilitate effective quarterly curriculum reviews. Such evidence would make the reviews meaningful and provide an incomparable, ongoing education for leaders themselves.

• Periodic or formative assessments—*with results achieved.* (For example, 77 percent of students succeeded on this essay, science project, unit test, or quarterly assessment, which assessed specific designated standards.)

- Grade books—with evidence that essential standards are being taught, and the number of students who are succeeding on these standards. (Explicitly including this information may require that grade book columns be more clearly labeled.)

- Team Lesson Logs or Learning Logs—with brief descriptions of lessons, units, and assessments being built and refined by teams—along with assessment results.

- Student work—for example, scored samples from key assignments. These samples provide incomparable, ongoing opportunities for *leaders to learn*—to understand and support instruction and assessment.

These reviews don't have to be time-consuming, or unpleasant. Nor do they have to be perfect. Good-faith attempts, by the average administrator, will send a strong message and have a serious impact on curricular quality and consistency. The effects will be especially strong if *leaders themselves work in teams*—using the same brainstorming and problem-solving strategies as teachers—to help one another become better at conducting these important reviews.

I have some firsthand experience here. Years ago, in one middle school where I taught, the principal met regularly with each teacher to conduct such a review. We were asked to bring our grade books. We English teachers brought one rubric-scored sample of student writing for each written assignment—with the student's rough draft. In these 15-minute meetings, the principal could see, in mere moments, the nature and number of our reading and writing assignments. She asked us fairly tame questions, such as: "Tell me about this assignment; how did it go?" "What elements of the rubric are kids struggling with, and how do we intend to improve in those areas?" These chats were short but exceedingly powerful. Unfortunately, most teachers will never have these types of regular conversations with their supervisors.

In addition, our principal made only occasional, brief visits to our classrooms. Within minutes, she could see if we were teaching to the agreed-upon curriculum. I can guarantee you that these very reasonable, time-efficient routines, in combination, had a powerful influence on the quality of our teaching and ensured a "guaranteed and viable curriculum" for students at the school. And it was obvious that the principal herself learned invaluable things at these meetings.

Any conscientious leader could be trained to conduct these reviews. This experience was decades ago; in a professional learning community, she might have conducted these reviews by team and saved even more time while giving us a chance to learn from each other. She might have met with individuals only if there were a problem or need. Department heads or directors might conduct these reviews, as they do at Adlai Stevenson High School and the Glendale Union High School District in Arizona (Schmoker, 2001b). In Johnson City, New York, the math department head at one high school, Dan Hendery, met with his teachers quarterly to review common assessment results. As a consequence of these simple meetings, the passing rate on the New York Regents exam increased from 47 percent to 93 percent—in a single year. No new program, no strategic plan brought these results, just leadership focused on common curriculum taught on a common schedule, guided by formative assessment results (Schmoker, 1999, p. 96).

At Boone's Mill Elementary School in Virginia, Principal Rebecca DuFour began to conduct such curriculum and assessment reviews with each team just four times a year, for an hour at a time. Teachers brought lists of essential standards they had taught that quarter, along with common team-made formative assessments and that quarter's results. They talked about these results, about samples of student work, and about what they would do to get better results on these assessments the next quarter. During a three-year period, the number of students succeeding at the highest levels on state assessments (given at two grade levels) tripled in one grade and doubled in the other. The percentage of students scoring in the top quartile on state-mandated norm-referenced tests increased from 27 percent to 50 percent (DuFour et al., 2004, p. 162).

At Adlai Stevenson High School, Rick DuFour met with teams or with his directors, who conducted these reviews with the teams themselves. The teacher teams came to these meetings with results from the common assessments they administered—given six to eight times per year in every course. DuFour told me that these assessments were the most time-efficient, precise way to monitor whether a consistent, viable curriculum was being taught. The directors also shared each team's evaluation of these results and their plans for improving performance in low-performing areas.

Eventually, DuFour and his directors found it helpful to review a breakdown of each team's major assignments along with the respective weight of the assignments in students' overall grades. Teams had to explain and justify their assignments and exams to ensure the right mix of objective testing and assessments of writing and higher-order reasoning.

The teams also reviewed grade-distribution data and failure rates, which allowed teachers to compare their success rates (anonymously) with those of their colleagues. This practice was invaluable. In a context where teachers shared common curriculum and assessments, this review reduced failures and helped teachers aspire to the highest rates on the team. On occasion, teams would group-score key projects and written assignments to stay sharp and ensure high, consistent standards.

Although fairly standard practice in other professions, such teamwork is radical stuff for educators. But as Lortie noted long ago, "The monitoring of effective instruction is the heart of effective instruction" (1975, p. 41). We must be willing to conduct such reviews in light of the immediate and positive impact such commonsense procedures would have on teaching quality and curriculum coherence.

How Do We Get There? Making the Case and Conducting Dialogue

As sensible and effective as such team structures and periodic reviews may be, they run right up against a culture that believes that monitoring isn't essential, that real professionals are best left alone. To establish new understandings and actions, we have to engage educators in dialogue as we share and consider the powerful, compelling case for these new team structures and leadership practices. If we lose our nerve here, we are only pretending to be serious about improvement.

We have to own up to the fact that we have often asked teachers, without much explanation or warning, to attend training sessions and commit to any number of feckless, unproven initiatives over the decades. Too many leaders were encouraged to view their "districts and schools as Christmas trees" and the "various education fads as ornaments" (Eaker, 2002, p. 27). The irony is that those who don't "buy in" are pejoratively labeled "resisters"—when they are only resisting initiatives that we had no business importing in the first place.

This time we have to do it differently. Leaders need to make a thorough, evidence-based case for effective instruction, for monitoring to ensure high-quality curriculum in every classroom. We have to lay out the incontrovertible evidence that shows that teachers are always more effective when they work in disciplined teams. We need to make this case and then allow for dialogue—for people to inquire and express reasonable disagreement as we work toward informed agreements and commitments to action.

In making this transition, DuFour had great success using a fairly formal dialogue process (which I've since had great success using; see the agreements in Appendix C). By all but eliminating after-school meetings, DuFour was allowed to meet with teachers in small groups during planning periods or lunch. Their dialogue began with DuFour

- Making the case for a change or initiative (for example, adopting fundamental elements of professional learning communities such as a common curriculum, teamwork, and common assessments).

- Providing reasoning, evidence, and concrete examples that argue for adopting the change (would that we had made *this* a requirement for adopting initiatives long ago).

- Acknowledging areas of uncertainty where teachers are invited to help the leader achieve clarity or solutions.

- Inviting others to question the leader's assumptions and conclusions.

Similarly formal processes were followed to allow the parties to thoroughly inquire and understand one another's thinking, for expressing disagreement, and for suggesting alternatives. But all dialogue was conducted with an emphasis on reason and evidence as the basis for reaching concrete, written agreements.

Importantly, administrators benefited greatly from hearing disagreements and alternatives to some of their ideas. Just as important, it was through this dialogue that the team formalized some crucial assurances for teachers:

- The professional learning community process will not require me to work beyond my contractual day.

- Results from common assessments will not be used in my evaluation in a punitive way.

- Results from common assessments will not be shared with others.

- I will be able to retain much of my individual autonomy in terms of instructional strategies and teaching style.

With these written agreements in place, the following commitments could now be made in an atmosphere of trust (adapted from DuFour, 2005 and personal communication with Richard Dufour, July 15, 2005):

- Students will have the benefit of educators who work collaboratively to
    - Ensure a common curriculum.
    - Seek out and refine practices that have the most positive impact on student achievement.

- Student work will be judged according to the same essential criteria across the department.

- Students will be provided with examples of quality work to help them learn and self-evaluate.

If any of these commitments were violated, the parties had the written documents as a recourse. These agreements served both teachers and administrators exceedingly well as Stevenson made its impressive march toward excellence. At Boone's Mill Elementary School, Principal Rebecca DuFour initiated such dialogue and discipline to establish the conditions for rapid, across-the-board achievement gains.

Such is the stuff of a culture of discipline. And these efforts illustrate the investment required for vastly better schools.

When Reason Becomes the Arbiter of Action

These processes served DuFour and Stevenson High School exceedingly well. Rick shared with me that almost without exception, these formal dialogue processes overwhelmingly favored the adoption of effective practices and the rejection of ineffective, current practices (the flimsy rationale for which becomes apparent in such discussions, especially when they are posted and in writing).

With the clear need for change amply supported by good sense, research, and examples of successful schools, we are asking schools to adopt elements like the following:

• A coherent curriculum, with the responsibility to teach *fewer* standards (while teaching them better and in more depth).

• A renewed commitment to teaching critical thinking and literacy—at the upper ends of Bloom's taxonomy *that we claim, rightly, to revere.*

• Evidence that most lessons contain the elements essential to success.

• Periodic classroom tours, predominantly intended to identify and report back to the faculty on schoolwide patterns of strength and weakness.

There is a clear, urgent need for such reasonable expectations to be adopted and put in writing. Dialogue, at every level, would surely advance this goal. If school leaders joined these expectations with immediate efforts to identify and celebrate every in-house, team-based success, any school or district could build trust, credibility, and momentum that would be hard to resist.

To put the need in perspective: we would be properly outraged if administrators routinely failed to show up for appointments with parents, or if most teachers frequently arrived at class 10 or 15 minutes late. But we tolerate practices that are at least as irrational—and egregious—when we fail to monitor or ensure effective instruction or a coherent curriculum that includes plenty of purposeful reading, writing, and critical thinking. We need to openly discuss and reckon with our historic inattention to such essential standards and practices. We don't tolerate doctors who fail to wash their hands before surgery. It is time for the education professions to develop a healthy amount of what Roland Barth calls "moral outrage at ineffective practices" (2002, p. 10).

Among leadership's most ineffective practices is teacher and administrative evaluation.

Teacher Evaluation: Nowhere to Go But Up

Teaching, despite its decisive and enduring impact on student learning, isn't meaningfully monitored or evaluated (Tucker & Stronge, 2005; Marshall, 2005). As Douglas Reeves and others have helped us see, the evaluation of administrators is equally as superficial (Reeves, 2002b). Evaluation seldom challenges the "prevailing norms of non-interference, privacy, and harmony" that prevent instructional improvement (Little et al., 2003, p. 187).

All of this should alarm us. In any profession, evaluation is an indispensable management tool—a critical component of quality control. In education, evaluation is currently a shambles. As Kim Marshall argues conclusively, the tradition of evaluating teachers on the basis of one or two observations is a farce. It constitutes "ridiculously thin supervision of the school's most important employees" (2005, p. 728). Even the least effective teacher can put a passable lesson together once or twice a year to satisfy an evaluator. But learning, as Marshall points out, depends on the quality of the other "99.7 percent of the time"—for which we lack even the most indirect evidence of good or poor performance.

The mind reels at how we allowed this essential management tool to devolve into irrelevance, with dismaying consequences for students and the teaching profession alike.

We are what we evaluate. What if teacher and administrative evaluation were recast around the fundamentals we've described? What if we assembled, in the most time-efficient fashion possible, satisfactory evidence that teachers are indeed

- Teaching, year-round, to a viable, agreed-upon curriculum that includes plenty of reading, writing, and critical reasoning.

- Working in teams to produce ever-improving, short-term assessment results.

We would have a revolution in the making.

Evaluation Owned by Teacher Teams

Both of these dimensions of performance could be evaluated via the curriculum review meetings just described. If teachers felt that their evaluations were unfair, an appeal process would not only be allowed but *encouraged,* as teachers sought clearer and more efficient ways to demonstrate—with grade books, assessments, and student work—that they were indeed teaching agreed-upon standards and producing effective lessons and assessment results with their colleagues. Remember that, unlike the often time-gobbling, questionable requirements of many career ladder programs, these practices would have an immediate and direct effect on achievement gains.

The case for linking some portion of evaluation to evidence of continuous attention to quality curriculum and effective practice is gaining ground. Kim Marshall advocates such a model—one that is "owned by teacher teams" (2005, p. 732). Teachers would be evaluated on work they do with colleagues—creating, assessing, and adjusting their instruction, in cycles, using "common interim assessments" that reflect attention to essential state standards (p. 733). He advocates that we evaluate teachers on the basis of their willingness to answer questions such as

> What percentage of students scored at the advanced, basic, or below-basic levels? In which areas did students do best, and where were they confused or unsuccessful? What is our strategy for

addressing the weakest areas and helping students who are struggling? (p. 733).

This approach doesn't require that we rush toward one-dimensional, test-based evaluation. It does require that we look hard at evidence that teachers are making good-faith efforts to work with their colleagues to improve performance on formative assessments that conform to an agreed-upon curriculum—all very reasonable stuff.

We need to build on existing pilot projects like those described in Tucker and Stronge's *Linking Teacher Evaluation and Student Learning.* Teachers are embracing these models, some of which are now paying off richly. Consider the Thompson school district in Loveland, Colorado, where the new evaluation system has resulted in the highest academic growth among Colorado's 176 school districts (Tucker & Stronge, 2005, p. 52).

We should be studying such districts closely: Thompson's evaluation criteria are right in line with the fundamentals I have described. The evaluation requires evidence of consistent (versus one-shot) attention to effective instruction; *multiple, unannounced* visits must reveal that lessons have a clear "initial focus . . . guided and independent practice, monitoring of instruction . . . formative and summative assessment." The "professional . . . analyzes the results of instruction and modifies instruction accordingly." And all teaching must be "consistent with state standards" and "the adopted curriculum" (Tucker & Stronge, 2005, p. 45).

These emphases, combined with higher levels of purposeful collaboration, have resulted not only in sizeable achievement gains but also in higher levels of teacher satisfaction and "a feeling of professionalism" (p. 50). Which brings us, almost naturally, to the more controversial issue of teacher compensation.

Leveraging Teacher Pay

> Sure, but there isn't a word here about the incentives and punishments needed to make teachers and schools *want* to have results!
>
> —Peter Drucker, commenting on
> *Results, the Key to Continuous School Improvement*

If teacher evaluation can be productively linked to better teacher performance and achievement gains—as it so evidently has in places such as Loveland, Colorado—then it is no great leap to consider that teacher evaluation linked to compensation would also lead to gains in achievement. Denver schools are a case in point. After a pilot project there, teachers union members approved a compensation system that includes incentives based on student growth and teacher evaluations (Jupp, 2005, p. 11).

According to Robert Gordon, John Kerry's education adviser, failure to restructure teacher compensation only postpones improvement:

> Strengthening teaching requires changes to the pay system and school culture that abet mediocrity . . . across the board pay hikes reinforce the irrelevance of achievement. (2005, p. 26)

Once again, like so many features of the current system, teacher compensation structures only *reinforce the irrelevance of achievement.* I'm sad to say that many merit-based or career ladder systems fall short. They keep teachers very busy but steer clear of monitoring authentic evidence of consistently delivered coherent curriculum and effective teaching. We could greatly accelerate efforts to improve schooling by moving to a compensation system that productively, if imperfectly, links pay to performance. Such schemes will never be perfect, but, as Collins stresses, this approach is "basically reasonable and rational" (2001a, p. 49).

The current system is neither reasonable nor rational. It allows the least effective tenured teacher in the district to earn two to three times as much as the most-effective—but new—teacher.

At the very least, annual raises could be made contingent on meeting the most obvious and powerful professional standards that we wrongly presume are now being met—namely, teaching a guaranteed and viable curriculum as a contributing member of a team working to improve instruction on the basis of formative assessment results. The new system could be that simple. Or it might include an incentive for exceptional contributions or exceptional results. Such simple changes would inject a much-needed dose of professionalism into teaching and the status of teachers.

Allen Odden is well-known for his excellent research in the area of performance pay for teachers; his work has been generously praised by leaders of both the National Education Association and the American Federation of Teachers (Odden & Kelley, 2002). Like so many studies we've mentioned here, his research points to the unavoidable fact that "improved classroom instruction is the prime factor to produce student achievement gains" (Odden & Wallace, 2003, p. 64). His studies also show that connecting teacher pay to performance could be one of the most powerful levers for promoting better classroom instruction, higher student achievement and, of vital importance, higher overall levels of compensation.

In "Leveraging Teacher Pay," Odden and Wallace point out that rewarding teachers for longevity and education units is simply "not linked to student achievement gains" (p. 64). On the other hand, research reveals that if we linked compensation to evaluation, achievement would "rise dramatically," and the achievement gap would shrink. Such compensation schemes force the system to take crucial elements more seriously: recruitment, selection, and teacher evaluation. And, to provide further incentive for change, existing experiments indicate that these forms of compensation lead *to higher overall levels of pay for teachers.*

Michael Fullan argues that educators, like other professionals, should not be afraid to enter the "quid pro quo world of delivering results to secure more resources" (2005, p. 35). Money talks. Linking compensation to evaluation would send a ringing message throughout the system: Because coherent curriculum and effective instruction are so manifestly vital to our children and their futures, these practices will be meaningfully evaluated—and rewarded. Schools will no longer wink at shoddy practice and curricular chaos while students' lives hang in the balance. This linkage would demonstrate, to teachers new or veteran, to governments and communities, that public education has acquired a higher level of competence and integrity. The price for this is oversight—and a willingness to make much-needed changes to how we evaluate and compensate teachers.

If we're smart, we'll make administrative evaluation an extension of teacher evaluation.

Leadership Evaluation: Wired for Failure

Here, too, there is nowhere to go but up. An excellent, practical, and forthright treatment of leadership evaluation is Douglas Reeves's *Assessing Educational Leaders*. In this book, he describes the "generally deplorable state" of leadership evaluation forms, which often resemble the state and district improvement templates from which they derive (Reeves, 2002a). These templates overflow with long, meaningless lists of ambiguously worded actions and objectives.

Wired for failure, these forms wreak havoc with clarity and focused action. If irrelevant activities count toward high marks on leadership evaluations, then leadership will be irrelevant. Reeves cites, for instance, an evaluation that asks principals to provide evidence that teachers are incorporating technology into instruction. Could anything be more ambiguous, more apt to promote token trainings or the most arbitrary use of technology—or (we've all seen plenty of this) misguided purchases of technology? (Collins calls this mindless enchantment with technology "the technology trap"; see 2001a, p. 154.) There may be great possibilities for improving instruction through the judicious, experimental use of technology. But I have yet to see a single technology objective linked tightly to assessment or based on achieved results, in language that requires leaders or practitioners to gauge the actual impact of specific lessons that incorporate technology. The point here is that we sanction thoughtless action when we build such requirements into leadership evaluations.

Reeves cites another evaluation template that requires principals to "participate in professional development activities." What does *this* mean? As Reeves points out, "my 4th grader's hamster can participate in professional development activities" (2002a, pp. 5–6).

This requirement tempts administrators to simply "meet" the objective by listing the presentations or conferences they have attended—irrespective of their impact on coherent curriculum or effective instruction. Forgive me, but I'm struck by how some administrators spend precious days attending conferences, year after year, *without ever implementing* what they learn at conferences they have already attended—without taking action to ensure more effective instruction or a guaranteed curriculum. Our leadership evaluations inadvertently encourage this.

Minimalist Leadership: Evaluate Only What Matters

Leadership evaluation doesn't have to be meaningless or time-consuming. It should be among our most vital, high-leverage tools for promoting improvement. It should reinforce and extend the same emphases found in the kind of teacher evaluation and team curriculum and assessment reviews already described.

For evaluation purposes, principals should be expected to document that teams at their schools have analyzed annual achievement data to set one or two measurable subject-area goals and to formally identify the lowest-scoring areas within those subject areas—where teams will concentrate their efforts (Schmoker, 1999, 2001a; Marshall, 2005).

Principals should then be able to document that each team has constructed a curriculum or standards map containing only the most essential learning outcomes for every course, and that each map is truly guiding instruction. Checklists and notes from monthly or quarterly curriculum and assessment reviews would be useful here.

Then principals need to look at evidence that teams are crafting and improving lessons and units together, adjusting their instruction on the basis of formative assessment results.

Leaders could document and share easy-to-gather evidence such as the following:

• **Schedules** for when teacher teams meet (and some indication of attendance at team meetings).

• **Protocols and team norms** that ensure that team meetings are productive—and *time-efficient* (one example—Effective Time-Efficient Meetings—can be found on pp. 119–20 in Schmoker, 1999).

• **Team lesson or unit logs** that help leaders to quickly and easily monitor and document information about teams and their progress, in mere minutes (these are indispensable to productive team meetings) (Schmoker, 2001b, p. 137).

- **Small wins recorded on the lesson or unit logs.** These wins should be recognized and celebrated at faculty meetings (more on this in a moment).

Such data—collected during, not at the end of, the school year—would become the new basis for central office discussions and problem solving and, by extension, the basis for the central office to evaluate its own performance. Such seamless attention to these matters at every level would influence the achievement of all schools within the district.

In sum, leadership evaluation should stop doing or abandon anything that doesn't have a manifest impact on the quality of what we teach or how well we teach. It should focus on finding the fastest, most productive ways to monitor and document evidence that leaders and teachers are truly focused on that small, fundamental set of actions with the highest impact on instructional quality. Such a focus on less, not more—combined with "simplicity and diligence"—is the key to improvement (Collins, 2001a) and is the antidote to sentimental notions of leadership that continue to hold us back.

The Tough Work of Instructional Improvement

Too much of the educational leadership literature is long on "harmony," "consensus," and sentimental, feel-good processes that float high above the hard, fundamental necessities of school leadership. Most especially, leaders need practical ways to monitor—and require—effective instruction and high-quality curriculum.

At its best, leadership is both "top-down" and "bottom-up"; it is "shared" (Lambert, 1998); it is "distributive" (Elmore, 2000). Even so, as Evans writes, "major change almost never wells up from the bottom. It begins near the top" (1996, p. 244). And because it confronts the most destructive elements of the status quo, it won't always or initially be popular. If we're serious about better schools, we must be "as bottom-up as possible; as top-down as necessary" (p. 245).

As we confront the status quo, we must enlist all professionals to this cause by sharing the strong, incontrovertible case for coherent curriculum and effective instruction, for team-based professional learning communities, and—very importantly—for the sensible, long-overdue leadership structures advocated here. As we make this case, leaders need to make room for reasonable objections and suggestions; we must arrange for teachers to experience and share small successes "early" and "often" (Hamel, as cited in Fullan, 2001, p. 33). If we work hard at these efforts, record numbers of average administrators will succeed, and we will win over unprecedented numbers of educators.

Nonetheless, not everyone will come along or come along immediately. I continue to work with schools where patent malpractice is blithely tolerated. Schools, like any effective organization, will need to be tougher, clearer, and uncompromising when essential, reasonable expectations aren't met. We must be willing, as Evans writes, to "raise appropriate guilt and anxiety" when the occasion demands (1996, p. 244). DuFour cites Daniel Goleman, well-known for his work on emotional intelligence, to make the point that sometimes dialogue, persuasion, and consensus aren't enough. Sometimes, it "simply comes down to using the power of one's position to get people to act" (DuFour, 2005).

Observers like Frederick Hess don't think that the tired culture of public schools is capable of such changes or decisive action (2004). Is this a fair criticism? Serious introspection is in order when, after two decades of reform, Judith Little and her colleagues lament that our culture of "non-interference, privacy, and harmony" continues to prevent teachers or leaders from getting around to "the tough work of instructional improvement." After two decades of reform, restructuring, and staff development, teacher talk rarely has an impact on instruction because teachers are still "rarely invited to look at evidence of student learning" (Little et al., 2003, p. 187). Surely we should know, by now, that this environment makes instructional improvement impossible.

Are most of our average teachers and leaders inclined to take on the tough work that will improve our schools and usher in our era of unprecedented effectiveness? I honestly don't know. If we think Hess and others are wrong, then it is time to prove it.

This undertaking won't be easy, but any school or district leader who is serious about improvement will be greatly helped by frequently employing an especially powerful, if rarely used, set of tools in the school leader's arsenal: reward, recognition, and celebration.

Reward, Recognition, and Celebration: No Longer an Option

In establishing a results-oriented culture, DuFour did one more thing with passion and strict regularity: he made occasions to reward, recognize, and celebrate accomplishments at every single faculty meeting and more formally at the end of each semester. He gave roses, plaques, or other items to teachers and teams for concrete, measurable achievements. This strategy turned out to be a powerful tool in promoting hard, smart work at Stevenson.

The case for recognition and celebration demands our attention, having emerged as one of the indispensable elements of effective leadership. Little includes it among the essential ingredients needed to foster and sustain productive collaboration (1987, p. 514). Tom Peters writes that high performance demands "unprecedented" levels of celebration and recognition. Great results require "obsessively" and "frequently" praising employees and sending thank-you notes, and creating multiple "public forums for recognition" each month (1987, pp. 305–313). He regards these occasions as the leader's most effective "teaching opportunities" and the "single most important opportunity to parade and reinforce the specific kinds of new behavior one hopes others will emulate" (pp. 308–309).

However, we mustn't be "promiscuous" with praise. Leaders should recognize only specific, legitimate accomplishments that move the school toward its goals. "Celebrate," cautions Peters, "only what you want to see more of" (p. 311).

Countless others agree. Reward, recognition, and celebration are at or near the top of every study of those factors that promote smart, enthusiastic work. Bob Nelson's studies found recognition and celebration to be the *number one* factor in promoting high performance (1994, p. xv). More recently, the Gallup database revealed that praise and recognition were among the top four factors essential to success; in the best organizations, the average employee received specific recognition or praise *at least once a week* (Buckingham & Coffman, 1999, pp. 28–29). This may be the single most powerful strategy for educational leaders who ask "How can we get buy-in and overcome resistance?" Educational researchers Blasé and Kirby found that praise and recognition for specific accomplishments was the most effective way to promote positive morale and productive behavior (1992).

As Robert Evan writes,

> The single-best, low-cost, high-leverage way to improve performance, morale and the climate for change is to dramatically increase the levels of meaningful recognition for—and among—educators. (1996, p. 254)

Do all these studies have our attention yet? Research and common sense point hard to the supreme importance of continuously recognizing and celebrating specific, short-term accomplishments that bring us closer to our goals.

Barriers to Praise

And yet there are serious cultural barriers here. In 1975, Dan Lortie described the "modesty of occasions" we provided for teachers to feel proud of their work. He found that education avoided recognition and praise—perhaps more than any other profession (p. 133). More recently, Evans found that recognition and celebration in schools "varies between meager and pitiful" and that we "shower recognition on pupils but deny it to adults" (1996, pp. 255–256).

We have to get past this barrier, which is a function of the egalitarian ethos that resists any practice that reveals or acknowledges the substantial differences between practices and practitioners. This resistance hurts both teachers and their students. As Evans points out, recognition and celebration are critical when we are asking for improvement: "When demand rises, support must rise proportionately" (p. 255).

Again, we mustn't be promiscuous with praise (Peters, 1987), but we should be aggressively liberal with it. We must spread it around as much as possible to counteract the initial resistance that teachers feel toward seeing their peers praised or recognized. Keep in mind that school people haven't yet learned to accept praise or to see its value for themselves or the organization. From the start, people should see that the focus is on celebrating and enjoying all the good things that happen in their midst, so that these can inspire further effective actions. The key is to be on the lookout for any legitimate effort or accomplishment that supports better teaching and learning:

- a willingness to work effectively in teams

- developing team norms and protocols (very important)

- a single effective, team meeting focused on instruction

- measurable success—or *instructive failure*—on an assessment of a single lesson or unit

We can even have colleagues nominate each other for legitimate efforts and accomplishments. Make no mistake, these practices are the bricks and mortar of real, life-changing school improvement. They will break down resistance and have a powerful effect on buy-in and morale.

Evans has advice for those afraid to take the plunge: just do it (1996). It is that important. In my experience, people quickly—almost immediately—come to greatly appreciate recognition and celebration. In two different districts where I worked, there was initial resistance to recognition and celebration—until we did it. People's responses were uniformly positive, and among my favorite memories as an administrator. I wrote a lot of thank-you notes and found, to my surprise, that most people appreciated any simple, tangible gift like those that Peters encourages. Even a free lunch at the school cafeteria (we had excellent faculty cafeterias) was welcome.

In one case, a free ticket to the movies—for volunteering to be a United Way site coordinator—contributed to our doubling payroll contributions that year. In another case, a department chair took the rather bold step of arranging for me to make a presentation to enlist English teachers for a team-based writing improvement pilot project.

My presentation was well-received, but only one teacher signed on. I sent the department head a thank-you note immediately—and a $5 gift certificate to a local bookstore for championing the project. When she received it, she called and told me, with some emotion, that in 30 years of teaching, no one had done anything like this (be ready to hear this from lots of people). "By the way," she added, "I enlisted six more people for the pilot project." The project went well, and it got good word-of-mouth, which led, in turn, to every other academic department developing common curriculum and assessments.

That is how we build momentum—by recognizing and celebrating each small win that brings us closer to providing consistent, quality curriculum, increasingly well-taught.

We can be confident that these few simple strategies will allow committed leaders to succeed at almost any individual school or district. But alas, only a very small proportion of schools and districts enjoy such success. Fear, overload, confusion—and inertia—still work mightily to prevent whole districts and states from making that first, tough turn of the "flywheel," to use Collins's now-famous metaphor. The first turn is the hardest. Large-scale improvement, truly within our reach, will require a new culture with new expectations—and an encounter with the brutal facts at the district and state levels. Success and clarity here may be our best hope for success at the national—and perhaps international—level.

10

Scaling Up

Central Office and State-Level Leadership in the Learning Community

> The real path to greatness, it turns out, requires simplicity and diligence. It requires clarity, not instant illumination. It demands each of us to focus on what's vital—and to eliminate all of the extraneous distractions.
>
> —Jim Collins

We've looked at leadership practices that would greatly improve teaching and learning in any school. Teachers and school leaders will succeed when they focus on what's vital, monitor it, and celebrate successes. Even a single team or a single school has the power to "create a pocket of greatness" Collins writes, without having to wait for the school, district, state, or provincial leaders "to get it" (Collins, 2001b, p. 104).

But don't we want more? Agreement among educators, researchers, and consultants on the effectiveness of these practices is no less than astonishing (see Appendix B). Shouldn't we wish to see these practices adopted on a state, provincial, or even national scale? Clearly, they haven't been, not even by low-performing schools that are right next door to dramatically improved schools and districts. Despite some small progress, a coherent curriculum and productive collaboration are still all too rare—even among those who have attended the right conferences, read the right books, and are well acquainted with the fundamental concepts of collaborative learning communities.

Why? One reason has to be that effective teaching and tough, instructionally focused leadership are still largely voluntary (Elmore, 2000). Changing the expectations, writes Fullan, will require that we firmly establish a new set of results-oriented "leadership standards . . . at all levels" (2005, p. 34).

If we wish to enter an era of unprecedented effectiveness, we must work to redundantly insist on and clarify, *at the district, state, and provincial levels,* these few, simple actions and concepts essential to better schools.

If we want to accelerate major improvement beyond individual schools, then districts must firmly establish new practices, policies, and job descriptions. If state or provincial departments can support—and mimic—these practices, we'll truly go to scale. But as Robert Eaker points out, it can be

> very difficult for an individual school to become a professional
> learning community if the district leader shows a different set
> of priorities, or priorities that are in another direction (in Eaker,
> DuFour, & DuFour, 2002, p. 82).

Like it or not, organizations are either supported or constrained by those who exercise authority at the next highest level. Many talented but tentative principals will be newly focused and emboldened where district leadership energetically and explicitly supports the work of professional learning communities (by whatever name).

In turn, exponentially more districts will succeed in states where leaders are encouraged and eventually required to embrace these same unequivocally effective practices.

If, as Deborah Meier writes, we "want to do it badly enough," if we truly wish to multiply the number of successful schools across the land, then we must replace current practices with concrete, common-sense actions at the central office and at the state or provincial departments of education. Leaders at these levels must also work in teams.

Teamwork at the District Office

Because of its influence on multiple schools, teamwork at the district level can pay off hugely. The primary work of the administrative team is to aggressively identify and systematically help to solve common problems that impede schools in their efforts to establish successful learning communities, for example:

- The team lesson or learning logs aren't coming in; most contain no assessment results; team meetings are still rambling and unproductive.

- Many teachers are resisting the requirement that they teach a common curriculum on even a roughly common schedule.

- The quarterly curriculum reviews are bogging down; teachers aren't bringing (or are pretending to forget?) grade books or student work.

- Some principals are struggling to get comfortable with recognition and celebration procedures; this is new terrain for them.

These problems are serious and, in my experience, inevitable. But the point here is that any diligent, focused team of administrators can generate solutions to such problems. The moment leaders begin to brainstorm for solutions on a flipchart, they will realize that many of these problems can be addressed with persistent efforts to clarify these new practices and their proven benefits, especially in the early going. We'll have additional success when we mobilize to provide immediate in-house assistance in areas of confusion or difficulty, and when we nourish progress by sharing any and every example of in-house success, however small. These are fairly straightforward actions, all of which will promote clarity and dispel confusion and resistance, which new practices always amplify.

Leaders will learn that with one another's help and ideas, they can make steady, meaningful progress on any of these fronts, while gaining confidence and momentum from frequently sharing small successes.

But these good things can't happen until we overhaul district office meetings.

District Office Meetings: Clarity, Priorities, and Persistence

> High-performing systems show that their leaders provide direction
> that is clear, strong, and unambivalent.
>
> —Robert Evans

In his 17th year as an administrator in New York, Anthony Alvarado made a penetrating observation: that he had sat through more than 150 administrative meetings where, he says, the discussions were "never about curriculum and instruction. It's turf, administration, budgets, and power." Alvarado knew this situation had to change, and change it did. District 2 became a place where "Everything we do in this district is geared toward the issue of teaching and learning" (Bradley, 1993, p. 1).

Although you'd never know it by attending most administrative meetings, they are exploding with opportunities to bring focus and clarity to schools. At one administrative meeting in a district where I worked, we finally took the time to clarify and establish what we meant by "goals." First, no more long-winded, ambiguously worded goals; they had to be measurable and linked to annual student assessments (e.g. "Math performance will increase from 47 percent to 52 percent on state/district assessment in 8th grade"). Then we capped the number of such goals at two per team—ending years of addiction to time-consuming annual improvement planning that guaranteed far too many goals and the overload and fragmentation that make improvement impossible (Fullan, 1996). This single half-hour agenda item at one administrative "team" meeting saved hundreds of hours of people's time and gave focus and clarity to our efforts for every school, every team, every teacher in the district. It contributed greatly to our district's highest achievement gains in years.

Most of the problems that stop effective learning communities in their tracks are similarly solvable—they are speed-bumps, not brick walls. In the same district, we began to focus our efforts on team-based instructional improvement to reach our (now-manageable)

measurable goals. A few schools and teams got underway immediately. One team decided to have regular meetings to work on writing
performance. Right away, team members experienced the usual problems and resistance, which could have brought the initiative down—
and would have in previous years.

But not this year. We still had a ways to go, but we made great
progress when we began to devote a generous portion of each central
office meeting to solving problems and clarifying the concepts essential to team-based continuous improvement. As soon as it was possible, we had successful teams share their short-term results. This sharing had a dramatic impact: principals left the meetings with greater
confidence and clarity about fundamental practices.

And nothing could have made the district office's commitment
clearer. We had finally developed what Evans calls a "predisposition
toward clarity" (1996, p. 215), an awareness that confusion always
leads to fear and misdirected effort. Any innovation must be described
and reinforced and modeled many, many times before we truly understand it. Our more conscious attempts to clarify and demonstrate
our commitment to team-based instructional improvement gave our
principals confidence and courage. This time, they understood the innovation, and they knew they weren't in it alone. They had the clear support of the district. And for the first time, they were given regular opportunities to see and hear about these very simple, focused practices—and
results—from successful teachers themselves.

As a result, team meetings at the schools became far more
focused and productive; some resembled pep rallies, as teachers high-
fived and applauded monthly gains. We were rolling. These successes,
at multiple schools, were a result of our administrative meetings,
which were, as Collins urges them to be, "frantically consistent with
our hedgehog concept" (2001a, p. 124). Collins's "hedgehog concept"
refers to the clearest priority—in our case, team-based, assessment-
driven instructional improvement

Team Meeting Protocols—Too Important to Overlook

We woefully underestimate how simplicity, redundancy, and clarity at the
district level inspire confidence and courage in building administrators.

This focus requires generous amounts of time at central office meetings where we maintain a "culture of discipline" (Collins, 2001a, p. 124). Strict team norms—meeting guidelines and protocols—are absolutely essential to this discipline. The norms must involve guarding the agenda, eliminating all but the most essential announcements, establishing time limits on discussion, and incorporating essential tools such as brainstorming. DuFour's administrative team developed clear but playful routines for letting administrators know when they were violating important norms—for instance, they wagged plastic rulers from their day-planners when someone got off task. Withal, we must guarantee that administrative team meetings devote sufficient time to discussing—and celebrating—instruction and its ongoing impact in the schools.

Central office meetings are really teaching opportunities for leaders to learn and be encouraged in the tough work of instructional improvement. These meetings could provide the single largest lever for promoting achievement throughout the district. This is sacred time: nothing can stop those who devote attention at every central office meeting to solving problems and sharing small wins as they mature into true learning communities.

Someone in the system has to have the primary (though not exclusive) charge to make sure that these essential processes and priorities get their due. This responsibility brings us to yet another truly ripe opportunity for better schools: the chance to redefine an underestimated, but exceedingly high-leverage position in the school district.

Redefine the Assistant Superintendent of Curriculum and Instruction

Inestimable benefits would result from redefining the assistant superintendent (or director or coordinator) of curriculum and instruction. Another great irony of public schooling is that the office of curriculum and instruction traditionally has so little influence on . . . curriculum and instruction.

This high-leverage position needs a thorough examination, and probably an overhaul. To the greatest extent possible, duties that have no palpable impact on curriculum and instruction should be eliminated—or passed on to other personnel. The new job description should align with the same emphases that have been enumerated here:

• Assemble the evidence and start the dialogue around the importance of common curriculum, common assessments, and the other fundamental elements of team-based learning communities.

• Coordinate the development, by teachers, of common end-of-course outcomes and assessments in every course and subject area, perhaps starting with areas tested on state exams.

• Establish procedures for grade and same-course teams to formally analyze annual achievement data, set measurable goals, and identify specific areas in need of improvement. (This is simple work; don't overcomplicate it. See "Demystifying Data Analysis," Schmoker, 2003.)

• Ensure that each school sets a schedule for teams to meet, and establishes effective team meeting protocols and procedures for documenting the team's focus and progress (e.g., team lesson or learning logs).

• Even a few times per year, take a team of teachers and administrators on a tour of randomly selected schools and classrooms. Provide a candid report to all administrators and schools on the patterns observed (standards were/weren't clear to students; plenty of/not enough evidence of thoughtful reading and writing). Four to six such one-hour tours and reports could work miracles. Then

　　○ Establish clear expectations for improvements the team will look for on the next tour.

　　○ Eventually, train personnel in each school (it's a snap) to conduct such tours.

• Continuously clarify effective team processes and have successful teachers model them at central office meetings. Recognize and celebrate short-term success at these meetings, and have successful teams provide brief presentations showcasing lessons and units that got great results. Encourage principals to do these same things at their faculty meetings. Just to be redundant: celebrate, celebrate, celebrate every short-term team success, *especially in the early going.*

- Annually review school performance data to identify particularly effective teachers and teams—your "positive deviants." Learn from them, give them opportunities to share their methods around the district or at lesson fairs—even if they're focusing on a single specific standard or set of outcomes.

If, in every district, someone had the clear charge to ensure that such things happened, it would have a seismic impact on instruction, improvement, and morale, on establishing a clear focus and a culture of discipline. It is high time that the duties of the position begin to match the title.

But this opportunity invites us to consider: if such simple, focused action will have such certain and immense benefits on whole districts, what will happen if these practices occur at the state level, and are reinforced and required by state-level officials?

A Plea to State Departments— for Clarity, Simplicity, and Support

When entire districts begin to support professional learning communities, record numbers of schools will succeed. When state education departments similarly clarify and simplify their requirements for schools, those schools will redirect time now wasted on extraneous distractions, such as those foisted on schools and districts by many state improvement templates. Change here will allow schools to invest their time and intelligence where it will make a historic difference for students—in ensuring a coherent curriculum and regular opportunities for teachers to continuously improve their instruction.

The entire apparatus of the state education department needs to move toward greater focus and simplicity. With a little imagination, they could develop simple, efficient ways to ensure that schools are teaching essential standards and providing effective instruction—by randomly visiting schools and asking for standards maps, quarterly assessment results, and samples of student work. The state's explicit focus and support for these fundamental priorities has to be incessantly communicated to district leadership and in turn to school leaders, many of whom are still confused by the unfocused array of tasks they are required to complete.

State departments have yet to see that such clarity, focus, and support from the state would embolden focused, productive action that many school and district administrators are hesitant to take in the current climate. Some administrators are so busy satisfying the multiple requirements of state planning and improvement documents that they never turn their attention to those few essential actions that have a direct effect on teaching and learning results—but aren't mentioned in state department requirements. This situation causes Doug Reeves to conclude, "With good policymakers and enlightened senior leadership, honorable choices do not subject a career to permanent jeopardy." But where we find "morally bankrupt" policies and "intellectually vapid senior leadership," many conscientious school personnel will continue to worship the false god of "compliance" (Reeves, 2002a, p. 34).

Harsh as it may sound, many of our state policies and requirements are neither intellectually nor morally viable. For decades, "compliance" has allowed schools to be busily occupied with "change" without achieving improvement. These policies have promoted fragmentation rather than focus, and ambiguity where clarity was desperately needed. This has given us schools that meet every bureaucratic requirement while failing to provide a viable curriculum and effective instruction, thus guaranteeing boredom, frustration, and the failure of students by the tens of millions.

This is a national tragedy; state education departments have an obligation and a rich opportunity to help turn this situation around.

Vision and Constructive Action at the State Department

State education department employees work extremely hard. But to overcome the "awful inertia of past decades" (Fullan, 2005, p. 32), new expectations need to be established through deliberate steps, such as conducting focused dialogue around these tough issues, starting internally, to establish written agreements that would refocus effort on the high-leverage, research-based actions that have been described here. These few simple actions and principles would get an immeasurable boost if we expand and refocus our written and oral communication at the state level—on an unprecedented scale. As we've seen, the case for more effective instruction and supervision, and for a more coherent, viable curriculum, is strong and readily available. If state education department newsletters and presentations repeatedly focused on this case and featured every in-state or provincial success that flows from more effective teaching and leadership, we would make progress at a record pace.

Like the best school districts, state education officials can take some of the same simple steps that would inspire a critical mass to take actions that would move us to scale. As a district-level administrator, I attended lots of presentations at the department of education. Why weren't a few minutes set aside at each such meeting to hear from teachers right within our state (I knew of several), whose exceptional accomplishments would have challenged us to realize that we could be vastly more successful with kids in even the poorest, most disadvantaged settings? There is nothing so compelling as live teachers who can describe how they helped exceptional numbers of students succeed. Every state—every district and school—has dozens, hundreds of such positive deviants among them.

Every state department field representative or trainer should be armed with simple stories of how ordinary, effective teaching—when focused on essential standards—will get remarkable results, just as it did for Sean Connors. Why not aggressively advertise these accomplishments in our newsletters and e-mailings? Why not create a new breed of demonstration sites based on effective instruction and exceptional results, not fancy programs or academies.

None of these steps are difficult or complex. Such actions could create a tipping point, a chain reaction in any state, and (with any luck) in other states as well, as more of them begin to succeed. Such a chain reaction happened to medical practice in Flexner's time, and it happened with great speed.

We have a moral obligation to take such actions in light of the predictable impact they would have on kids, on our horrific and unnecessary achievement gap, on critical reasoning and intellectual development. If we won't, then we don't deserve to be the stewards of this most important institution.

The same goes for our administrator preparation programs, which could have, I believe, an equally prodigious influence on thought and action at every level.

Administrator Preparation: An Opportunity

Perhaps the most direct and powerful impact of the Flexner commission was felt at the university level—where doctors were trained. Of the hundreds of medical schools that commission researchers studied, only one was found adequate to equip medical professionals for their work. The rest were poor, and most were "utterly hopeless" (Clarfield, 2004, p. 1).

We should be disturbed, then, by a large-scale study conducted by Columbia Teachers College, among the most prestigious schools of education in America. The Education Schools Project studied 28 representative administrator preparation programs from around the country. *Education Week* called the study a "damning assessment of the programs that prepare most of the nation's principals and superintendents." Even those programs claiming to have made major improvements were found to have "little connection to the realities of running a school or district" (Archer, 2005, p. 1). According to Arthur Levine, who led the study, most programs are "little more than a grab-bag of survey courses" (in Archer, 2005, p. 2). The only institutions they could recommend were in Britain.

The response to these brutal findings warrants some hope. The presidents of the National Association of Elementary School Principals and National Association of Secondary School Principals immediately affirmed the study's conclusions, agreeing that administrator preparation programs "fall woefully short" of what is needed to improve schools (Tirozzi & Ferrandino, 2005, p. 12). Many observers are predicting that this study will have a major impact on how we prepare administrators.

A Lack of Focus

Interestingly, the study found that the "key problem" with these programs "is a lack of focus" (Archer, 2005, p. 2). Frederick Hess, pondering the findings, wonders why, after years of watching the machinery of accountability emerge, we did so little to prepare future school leaders for the rigors of "managing for results" (Hess & Kelley, 2005, p. 36).

Imagine if we did, if both undergraduate teaching and leadership preparation took this opportunity to provide courses with a clear focus on those few principles and practices that would transform our schools: the simple, powerful rudiments of professional learning communities that so many professors and researchers have endorsed for decades.

We could begin by telling the difficult truth about curriculum and instruction in administrative coursework; by incessantly sharing stories and cases of successful schools; and featuring teachers and leaders as guest speakers who can demonstrate the power of a coherent curriculum, of focused teamwork that produces a stream of successful lessons and units—which we must continuously honor, recognize, and celebrate.

We could much more aggressively share the manifold benefits such actions would bestow on our children and society. (What could we predict in a nation where the dropout rate and the achievement gap were reduced by half and where college graduation rates increased by an appreciable percentage? Even conservatively, how would this change affect social equity, crime rates, social pathologies, and prosperity?)

We could train administrators to learn the importance of redundancy, clarity, and simplicity; they could learn to engage in dialogue on the pivotal issues and actions that lead to collective commitments to foster continuous instructional improvement. Administrators could be taught to coordinate the development of common assessments, to conduct quarterly curriculum and assessment reviews, to conduct brief classroom tours, and to effectively and tactfully share patterns of strength and weakness with their faculties. The opportunities are ripe to have a truly significant impact on the effectiveness of the great majority of administrators.

These are the big levers of leadership that guarantee results. But I know very few educators, including those with doctorates, who have had opportunities to learn such practices. Few have read and discussed the evidence that points quite clearly to this untapped opportunity we have to close the achievement gap, to promote learning, literacy, critical reasoning, and a much richer, more interesting school experience.

Administrator preparation programs are in a uniquely powerful position to radically alter current practices and expectations, to positively and powerfully affect how leaders lead and teachers teach in every state or province, district, and school.

At the state, university, district, and school levels: what are we waiting for?

Conclusion

Why Not Us? Why Not Now?

There are a lot of children who are suffering, and we should not have to wait another generation before we get things right.

—Rev. Michael Pfleger

Education is the most powerful weapon which you can use to change the world.

—Nelson Mandela

The Scandal of Delay

With so much at stake, is there any decent reason to postpone what could be education's greatest moment? Does it make any sense for teachers to continue working alone, and therefore less effectively? For students to attend schools where instruction is largely unsupervised? Where "curriculum"—good or bad—depends largely on which teacher your child happens to get? Should we continue to deny tens of millions of students the opportunity to read and write and learn in ways that engage the intellect—while their enthusiasm for learning, their intellectual and career prospects suffer irretrievably?

In the wake of the Flexner report, medical professionals did not wait or delay or make excuses for the gap between professional and actual practice. They acted, immediately, in response to the brutal facts. Their response allowed generations of people to live longer, healthier lives.

As I've pointed out, the major impetus for writing this book was that the research and observations cited here resonated so strongly with audiences of educators and the small groups I met with. When we closely and honestly examined these facts, a clear majority agreed that we are woefully short of meeting even quite reasonable expectations in the areas of curriculum, literacy, critical reasoning, and leadership. They recognized that our failure in these areas ensures that far too much classroom instruction is mediocre—or worse. And they acknowledged the consequences of these shortcomings on students and their learning, their lives.

If the current school system wishes to survive against the increasing encroachments on its autonomy, perhaps its very existence, then there is only one worthy course of action: for teachers and school leaders at the state or province, district, and school levels to immediately and relentlessly begin to share, examine, and engage in dialogue about these realities on every occasion—until our actions and commitments begin to erase the awful inertia of past decades.

Like the tipping point that occurred in the medical profession, education has a historic opportunity to respond to these brutal facts with the simple actions that will swiftly and substantively improve our schools for all children, regardless of birth or circumstance.

For millions of children, we can change the world. Let's start this school year.

Appendix A

Suggestions for Teaching Critical and Argumentative Literacy

The purpose of this appendix is to briefly reiterate some of the key themes treated in Section II and to provide some practical suggestions, questions, and topics that can guide productive reading, writing, and discussion in various subject areas.

Argumentative Literacy

As we saw in Chapter 6, a focus on helping students acquire argumentative literacy has manifold benefits—for helping students think and read critically and write effectively. We saw how Hillocks's work suggests that students do their best writing in the argumentative mode (1987). We can regard the best reading standards as invitations to argue—to defend or support a claim about an interpretation, an author's purpose, bias, or credibility; to defend conclusions we draw; or to distinguish between facts and opinions (which often masquerade as facts) as we argue for or against the claims or inferences in the texts we encounter.

Gerald Graff provides a useful format for helping students to read and write critically and argumentatively. It can be used for virtually any integrated reading/writing assignment. These simple steps constitute the essence of intellectual and academic inquiry, for school or for life:

Argumentative Writing Template

• Read a text or texts very carefully (as often as possible, select texts with differing or opposing viewpoints).

• Based on your reading, make a claim—and make the claim *very clear* to your reader.

• Summarize objections to your claim.

• Make one point at a time, supporting your claim and addressing the objections.

• Write clearly enough so that *virtually anyone* can understand what you have written. (Graff, 2003, pp. 275–277)

Such a simple format can be adapted to write anything from editorials to literary criticism to research papers.

The Magic of Imitation

> Writing is learned by imitation. I learned to write mainly by reading writers who were doing the kind of writing I wanted to do.
>
> —William Zinsser (1988, p. 15)

Mike Rose learned to write by imitating "the styles of Conrad, Hemingway, and *Time Magazine*" (1989, p. 33). Composition theorist Frank D'Angelo cites a raft of great writers who emphatically claim that they acquired their own prose style by consciously imitating writing they admired (1980, p. 426). I've seen how average students can produce surprisingly effective prose by imitating powerful, vivid selections from literature or nonfiction. Students might be invited to carefully read and discuss the structure and power of Martin Luther King's inspiring "I Have a Dream" speech—or a portion of it—and then write their own short or long adaptation for a dream or aspiration of their own.

We might have students imitate descriptive literary passages such as this prose poem that is the opening of John Steinbeck's *Cannery Row:*

> Cannery Row, in Monterey, in California is a poem, a stink, a grat-
> ing noise, a quality of light, a tone, a habit, a nostalgia, a dream.
> Cannery Row is the gathered and scattered, tin and iron and rust
> and splintered wood, chipped pavement and weedy lots and junk
> heaps. . . .

You can feel the power in this gloriously imitable passage. It continues, with varying sentence styles, for almost a page—as he paints
numerous word-pictures of the inhabitants of this rough, noisy but
ultimately poetic setting—a place Steinbeck loved dearly. Students
could imitate (or even parody) such passages, while describing their
own town or a place they love; while "trying on" this poem's style and
inventive use of metaphors.

Or look at this opening to an opinion piece written by a local
journalist urging people to reject an additional big-box store in the
town I live in:

> Independent businesses have faced a tough road over the last 15
> years. Tens of thousands have closed as chain retailers such as
> Home Depot, The Gap, and Barnes and Noble have multiplied.
> Biggest of all is Wal-Mart, which now has 3,000 stores in the U.S.,
> commands nearly 9 percent of all retail spending, and accounts for
> one-tenth of our trade deficit with China (Mitchell, 2004).

How's that for a power-packed lead? Students will note the ominous
tone and build-up, the effective use of language: "tough road" (nice
use of vernacular); "tens of thousands" and "commands" with con-
notations of (perhaps inordinate) power in the marketplace. They
might note the use and position of "Biggest of all" at the end of this
litany of corporations. An excellent rejoinder to this piece—by col-
umnist George F. Will—can be found at http://www.msnbc.msn.
com/id/5304839/site/newsweek.

Writing (and Reading) Instruction

First, as Zinsser writes, "the essence of writing is rewriting" (1988, p.
15). Opportunities for significant revision—to form and content—are
absolutely essential (Hillocks, 1987; Zinsser, 1988). As Hillocks found,

students need to write whole drafts before they know what they want to say and how to organize their work. When students prematurely attempt to write first drafts while focusing on the paper's final form, they "short-circuit" the writing process. Attempting to write a final draft as the first draft blocks effective thought, and the student is then "unable to produce arguments of high quality" (p. 73).

And we need to get over our sometimes subtle aversion to using rubrics and scoring criteria more systematically. As the Learning 24/7 study indicates, too many teachers—even those who claim to find them useful—don't use scoring guides enough or teach each element *explicitly and repeatedly* (Learning 24/7, 2005). Students need to be consulting their criteria throughout the writing process; they need samples—exemplars—of student and professional written work that illuminate these criteria as nothing else can.

As Deborah Meier points out, our failure here is calamitous. When we fail to carefully and explicitly explain, model, illustrate, and provide examples of the kind of work we expect, we are not being "creative." We are in fact only "withholding secrets from the minority students [how about *all* students?] who most need" these skills. Speaking specifically of our failures in the areas of reading, writing, and thinking, Meier expresses her bafflement with our "avoidance of 'direct' instruction, as though if we waited long enough, children would discover everything on their own" (in Graff, 2003, p. 266).

The Paper Load: Write More, Grade Less

Here is truly a knowing-doing gap. If we close it, we'll launch the "writing revolution" from which all our students would so greatly benefit—without burdening teachers.

Briefly, it is not practical or beneficial to spend time writing numerous comments on students' papers. This practice wastes teacher time, is counterproductive, and has the opposite of its intended effect. Worst of all, it results in teachers assigning less writing, as each assignment portends untold hours of burdensome paper-grading.

A drastic shift and a new awareness are needed here. As Anne-Marie Hall advises, "Write more; grade less" (1994). The research is strong that students are far better off when we score their work for only one or two criteria that we have just finished teaching carefully and explicitly—and with the help of exemplars that add immensely to our best attempts to describe or define "voice" or "effective transitions" or "thoughtfully placed details" in a paragraph. Students need limited amounts of specific feedback—and they need it quickly, with the opportunity to correct or revise.

Marzano and others have shown that we can be vastly more effective while spending only a fraction of the time we now spend on grading (see link below). It comes down to how we structure writing or, more accurately, reading/writing assignments. We will have much greater success if we greatly increase amounts of writing while scoring for only one or two criteria at a time; when we have students complete their writing in stages, with brief conferences with the teacher at critical junctures (on in-school writing workshop days). These stages can include prewriting, free-writing, establishing a working argument or thesis; or a rough *(working, flexible)* outline. And we will also save time and increase effectiveness by eliminating much of the traditional objective testing that now consumes so much teacher time and adds no value to students' authentic literacy skills.

For the research on this important area and a wealth of practical suggestions on how to reduce the paper load, go to http://mwp01. mwp.hawaii.edu/resources/qt-paperload.pdf. In this important area, teams are essential—team members can help one another find and refine methods that increase the quality of literacy instruction while reducing time spent providing it.

Questions, Topics and Prompts for Meaningful Reading, Writing, and Discussion Across the Disciplines

As Postman (1969, 1997), Sizer (1992), Wiggins and McTighe (1998) and others have averred, the essence of an effective education is built around good questions. Good topics and prompts are the best opportunities to learn inquiry—questions in a different form. For example, we might ask students to read two opposing texts and then write a synthesis in which they "defend or criticize the construction of the wall on the West Bank in Israel" (there are plenty of good opinion pieces on this topic on the Internet). This is only another way of posing the question: "Was the West Bank wall a good or bad idea on the part of the Israeli government?"

I have placed these questions and prompts in what I hope are helpful, if somewhat arbitrary categories. They are not pure; their contents overlap. And I do believe that English or language arts will benefit by pulling texts from several of these categories, including nonfiction as well as literature. I have organized them in this way so that we can see the opportunities that emerge when we think in these modes. Marzano has certainly shown us how teaching via "compare and contrast" or "identifying similarities and differences" can promote exceptionally high levels of intellectual engagement and learning (Marzano, Pickering, & Pollock, 2001, pp. 14–15). Variations on this method can be used repeatedly for limitless assignments. As Mike Rose writes, praising the importance and usefulness of compare and contrast:

> Knowledge in the arts and sciences is gained by methodically examining one object or event or theory in relation to another. . . . Entire disciplines . . . are built on this intellectual strategy. . . . I wanted to give [students] the chance to develop confidence and facility in comparing points of view and explanations. (1989, p. 139)

These topics, prompts, and questions are, of course, only suggestions, intended to be used or adapted—or to spur other or better questions or prompts for effective critical and argumentative reading, writing, and discussion. The best prereading prompts and questions will, of course, be generated by teams, whose best questions should be regularly shared throughout the school and system to multiply their impact on lessons and literacy instruction.

Note that all of these "writing" assignments are really reading/writing assignments. They require close reading, or rereading—with "pen in hand"—to underline, take notes, or complete a graphic organizer. And consider how much more engaging and enduring the learning of content would be if taught in this fashion. (I often wonder if students wouldn't learn and retain and enjoy learning at far higher levels if we sought to find ways to teach virtually all subject-area content—

100 percent of it—in the inquiry mode; even lectures can be conducted in the inquiry mode).

Social Studies, History, Economics, Science

USA Today frequently runs very readable same-day, pro-con pieces on major issues in its op-ed page. This great resource can be searched from the Archives section on the *USA Today* Web site at www. usatoday.com.

- Evaluate or compare as the best, favorite, or greatest:
  - President (any two or more, in general, or for war-time, economic or other aspects of leadership)
  - Space mission (first orbit of the earth, the moon, space station, Mars exploration)
  - Economist (Keynes or Friedman? arguably the most influential economists ever)
  - Civil Rights leader (Harriet Tubman or Sojourner Truth? Martin Luther King Jr. or Malcolm X or . . . ?)

- Which woman made the most significant positive or negative contribution to the women's movement? Be sure your argument includes references to her rivals for this distinction (e.g., Susan B. Anthony and Betty Friedan)

- Evaluate or rank the relative contributions of scientists to the following areas of research:
  - Meteor Crater in northern Arizona (G. K. Gilbert, D. M. Barringer, or Eugene Shoemaker). [I had great luck with this assignment.]
  - Particle physics: the discovery/development of the atom (Ernest Rutherford; Niels Bohr; Werner Heisenberg)
  - Medical breakthroughs in cancer, heart disease, or HIV/AIDS
  - DNA (Watson, Crick, or others whose work formed the basis of Watson and Crick's discoveries)

- Defend the purchase of a stock or bond, relative to other stocks or bonds.

- Compare and contrast two countries (perhaps on different continents) for the following:
  - quality of life
  - economy
  - political maturity/freedom

- Opinions—for or against (wherever possible, provide texts for both sides of these issues):
  - The New Deal
  - The Contract with America (1994)
  - The 1960s War on Poverty
  - The wisdom of the United States entering WWI/WWII/ Viet Nam War/Iraq War
  - Breeding cows for veal
  - Big Box stores—bane or benefit?
  - Israeli withdrawal from Gaza
  - The South in the Civil War (aka "War of Northern aggression") (Ted Sizer once told me that every student should be required to write a paper arguing for the Southern perspective in the Civil War.)
  - The Israeli Wall

- From the 2004 Bush/Kerry presidential debates, compare and contrast the respective responses to selected debate questions (debate transcripts are available at http://www.msnbc.com/id/6146353).

Literature: Elementary and Intermediate Grades

Most of these are prereading questions—intended to guide and animate the critical faculties as students read, reread, and underline or take notes.

- In "Jack and the Beanstalk," evaluate Jack's character. Is he admirable or heroic? Or something else entirely? (The Junior Great Books program has lots of other good provocative texts and suggested questions.)

- In the folk tale "Hungry Spider and the Turtle," who would make a better friend, Spider or Turtle? (from Allington, 2001, p. 8)

- In *Green Eggs and Ham,* why is Sam so persistent? Do you like him? Is such persistence a strength or a shortcoming?

- Read "The Three Little Pigs" and then *The True Story of the Three Little Pigs by A. Wolf.* Argue for whose side you are on.

- Compare and contrast
  - "City Mouse and Country Mouse" for their attitudes and values.
  - "Sleeping Beauty" and Jane Yolen's *Sleeping Ugly* for what these say about inner and outer beauty.

- In "Goldilocks and the Three Bears," do you approve of Goldilocks's behavior? Can you appreciate or understand the bears' reactions to her intrusion?

Literature: Intermediate and Middle School

- Choosing characters from the following books, compare and contrast for courage/character, intelligence, and resourcefulness:
  - Old Dan and Little Anne in *Where the Red Fern Grows*
  - *Julie of the Wolves*
  - *My Side of the Mountain*
  - *Island of the Blue Dolphins*
  - *Hatchet*

- Compare and contrast the characters Ramona Quimby and Laura Ingalls Wilder from their books.

- In *Sarah Plain and Tall,* what are the pros and cons of Sarah's leaving to live with another family in the Midwest? (This one comes from a presentation given by Robert Swartz, whose work in the area of controversy-based learning can be found online at the National Center for Teaching Thinking: http://www.nctt.net/.)

Literature: Middle and High School

- Is Zeus just?

- Are the characters in *The Great Gatsby* happy? Why? Why not? Why do you think Tom Buchanan cheats on Daisy? What does the book say about America or the 1920s?

- In Jack London's *To Build a Fire,* do you admire the main character, based on his thoughts and actions?

- In *Julius Caesar,* was Brutus an honorable man?

- After reading *Of Mice and Men,* defend or condemn George's decision to kill Lennie.

- In Emily Dickinson's "Because I Would Not Stop for Death," what impressions do her thoughts and images make on you? Are they dreary? Hopeful? Positive? What might the poem say about the New England of her time?

- In Hemingway's (very) short story, "Cat in the Rain," what can you surmise about the characters from their dialogue and actions? Is this a healthy/unhealthy relationship?

Policy Proposals

- A better steroid policy for professional baseball (compare to NBA/NFL/NHL/Olympic policies).

- Middle East peace agreement (see "Forging a Lasting Middle East Peace" in Hess, 1999, for an excellent adaptable process for conducting such investigations).

- Where should we invest our energy dollars: in wind, solar, coal, or nuclear sources? What factors should we consider?

- Regulating multinational corporations (Starbucks, Wal-Mart, Nike, Microsoft).

- A humane but practical policy for managing prairie dogs in communities where they destroy crops.

- For any controversial topic, read an article from *National Review* or the *Weekly Standard* (conservative opinion journals) and one from the *Nation* (liberal) or the *New Republic* (center-left). Write your own opinion, synthesis, solution, or proposal on the basis of your reading.

Miscellaneous

Compare and contrast two or more, arguing for best, favorite, or greatest—there are excellent texts and statistics on all of the following:

- NASCAR drivers

- NFL quarterbacks

- NBA/NHL/MLB players

- Pop stars or rock bands—for example, the Rolling Stones have often billed themselves as the "world's greatest Rock and Roll Band." Do you agree? Would the Beatles have a better claim? On what basis?

Appendix B
Start Here for Improving Teaching and Learning

For all the current controversy surrounding issues of student achievement and accountability, we forget there is far less controversy about a shared desire on all sides to see more kids learn, to reduce the achievement gap, and to improve the quality of the complex work of teaching in all schools whether they are affluent or not.

So what if there was, right now, a fairly straightforward, well-established way to appreciably improve both teaching quality and levels of learning? What if evidence from numerous schools, as well as a broad concurrence of the research community, points to proven structures and practices that (a) stand to make an immediate difference in achievement and (b) require reasonable amounts of time and resources?

The fact is such structures and practices are at hand—and there's no reason to delay their implementation.

Rare Agreement

This simple, powerful structure starts with a group of teachers who meet regularly as a team to identify essential and valued student learning, develop common formative assessments, analyze current levels of achievement, set achievement goals, and then share and create lessons to improve upon those levels.

Picture these teams of teachers implementing these new lessons, continuously assessing their results and then adjusting their lessons in light of those results. Importantly, there must be an expectation that this collaborative effort will produce ongoing improvement—and gains in achievement.

If there is anything that the research community agrees on, it is this: The right kind of continuous, structured teacher collaboration improves the quality of teaching and pays big, often immediate, dividends in student learning and professional morale in virtually any setting. Our experience with schools across the nation bears this out unequivocally.

The concurrence on this is both stunning and under-appreciated. Advocates for focused, structured teacher collaboration include Roland Barth, Emily Calhoun, Linda Darling-Hammond, Richard Elmore, Michael Fullan, Bruce Joyce, Judith Warren Little, Dan Lortie, Milbrey McLaughlin, Fred Newmann, Susan Rosenholtz, Rick Stiggins, James Stigler, Joan Talbert, Gary Wehlage, Grant Wiggins, Ronald Wolk, and numerous others.

Darling-Hammond, a professor of teaching and teacher education at Stanford University, speaks for a legion of researchers when she writes that improvement is a function of "continual learning groups" pursuing "collective . . . explicit goals for student learning." She rightly emphasizes that success need not hinge on a school's luck in finding that rare administrator with charisma. It does, however, depend on collaborative "structures for success that maintain a press for ambitious teaching and academic achievement."

Similarly, Fullan, a newly appointed education advisor to the provincial government in Ontario, writes that teachers in successful schools form professional learning communities. They work together "on a continuing basis . . . focused on student work (through assessment)." On the basis of their assessment results, teachers then strategically "change their instructional practice accordingly to get better results."

Researcher Judith Warren Little's landmark studies on this topic are definitive. But they contain an important caveat: What passes for collaboration or collegiality in schools typically lacks a focus on achievement results—on short-term, formative assessment—and thus has very little impact on the character and quality of teaching. Educators must not confuse mere congeniality or "collaboration lite" with the serious professional dialogue essential to school improvement.

But, like Fullan and Darling-Hammond, Little found that when teachers engage regularly in authentic "joint work" focused on explicit, common learning goals, their collaboration pays off richly in the form of higher quality solutions to instructional problems, increased teacher confidence, and, not surprisingly, remarkable gains in achievement.

Concerted Action

Mere collegiality won't cut it. Even discussions about curricular issues or popular strategies can feel good but go nowhere. The right image to embrace is of a group of teachers who meet regularly to share, refine and assess the impact of lessons and strategies continuously to help increasing numbers of students learn at higher levels.

This image has yet to become the norm in most schools, despite the fact there are almost no dissenting entities on this issue, despite the contribution such joint work makes to teacher efficacy and professionalism, despite the fact it is neither costly nor time-consuming.

There is no good reason to delay this reform. It is time for a concerted press for its inclusion in state department requirements, in every preservice and leadership training course, and every discussion among principals and teacher leaders that purports to improve teaching and learning.

Indeed, other factors affect achievement. But continuous, organized opportunities for collaboration and assessment that are part of an ongoing cycle of continuous improvement allow us to make the most of the best factors and strategies. These structures offer us our most practical and affordable opportunity to integrate, generate, and refine practices that influence teaching learning.

The stakes are high, but success could redefine public education and the education professions. It could enable us to reach unprecedented levels of quality, equity, and achievement.

The author acknowledges the contributions of Richard DuFour, Carl Glickman, and Douglas Reeves in preparing this column.

Source: From "Guest Column: Start Here for Improving Teaching," by Mike Schmoker, November 2004, *The School Administrator,* pp. 48–49. Copyright 2004 by the American Association of School Administrators. Reprinted with permission. This text also appeared as the foreword to *On Common Ground: The Power of Professional Learning Communities,* edited by Richard DuFour, Robert Eaker, and Rebecca DuFour (2005; National Educational Service).

Signatories

Roland Barth is an author, educational consultant, and the founder and former director of Harvard University's Principal's Center and International Network of Principal's Centers (RSB44@aol.com).

Louis A. Castenell Jr. is dean and professor, College of Education, University of Georgia, Athens (lcastene@coe.uga.edu).

Lisa D. Delpit, eminent scholar and director, Center for Urban Education & Innovation, Florida International University, Miami, Florida (delpitl@fiu.edu).

Rebecca DuFour is an author and educational consultant on professional learning communities (mzprinci@charter.net).

Richard DuFour is an author and educational consultant on professional learning communities (rdufour@district125.k12.il.us).

Robert Eaker is an author and educational consultant on professional learning communities (reaker@mtsu.edu).

Barbara Eason Watkins is an author and chief education officer in the Chicago Public Schools (bewatkins@cps.k12.il.us).

Michael Fullan is an educational consultant, author, and the former dean of the Ontario Institute for Studies in Education of the University of Toronto (mfullan@oise.utoronto.ca).

Carl D. Glickman holds the Roy F. and Joann Cole Mitte Endowed Chair in School Improvement at Southwest Texas State University (isedinc@aol.com).

Asa G. Hilliard III is the Fuller E. Callaway Professor of Urban Education at Georgia State University (Ahilliard@gsu.edu).

Stephanie Hirsh is the deputy executive director, National Staff Development Council (NSDCHirsh@aol.com).

Jacqueline Irvine Jordan is Candler Professor of Urban Education at Emory University in Atlanta (jirvine@learnlink.emory.edu).

Lawrence W. Lezotte is an author and the founder of Effective Schools Products, Ltd. (www.effectiveschools.com).

Robert J. Marzano is an author and private consultant in Aurora, Colorado (robertjmarzano@aol.com).

Douglas B. Reeves is the chairman of the Center for Performance Assessment (DBReeves@aol.com).

Jonathon Saphier is an author and the founder and chairman emeritus of Teachers 21 and the founder and president of Research for Better Teaching (Jonathon1@aol.com).

Dennis Sparks is an author and the executive director of the National Staff Development Council (SparksNSDC@aol.com).

Rick Stiggins is an author and the chief executive officer and founder of the Assessment Training Institute (ati@assessmentinst.com).

Tony Wagner is codirector of the Change Leadership Group at the Harvard Graduate School of Education and Education Chair of the Harvard Seminar on Redesigning American High Schools (tony_wagner@harvard.edu).

Arthur E. Wise is the president of the National Council for Accreditation of Teacher Education (art@ncate.org).

Appendix C
Agreements

The following are agreements reached over a two-day period by an English department I worked with. All were reached through dialogue: it began with the department chair and me making the case for these policies and practices and then very formally inviting feedback, questions, disagreements, and suggestions from members of the department.

English Department Agreements

- Commitment to using two-thirds of class time for reading/writing/discussion of texts.

- Commitment to focusing on "power" [most essential] reading and writing standards.

- Commitment to emphasizing higher-order thinking through open-ended questions, argument, inquiry, and reasoning (two-thirds of class time). Whenever there are obstacles to teaching higher-order thinking, we will work as a department to overcome these obstacles.

- Commitment to clearly identifying the focus and standards to be learned in each lesson. Students learn better when they know from the start what they are trying to learn (the end goal).

• Commitment to having English department teachers gather each quarter and review the percentage of students who meet or exceed satisfactory levels of achievement on reading and writing quarterly assessments for the purpose of gauging and improving instruction. Instructors will work to develop common criteria for evaluating critical reading and writing proficiency.

Reading

• Commitment to teaching 8 to 10 books or novels in each course.

• Commitment to providing challenging, provocative questions about readings.

Writing

• Commitment to emphasizing
  o Persuasive writing (and well-supported arguments).
  o Real-world writing (e.g., grant applications).
  o Engaging, thought-provoking writing.
  o Writing based on close reading of one or more texts.
  o Varied writing applications and assignments (including literary analysis).

• Commitment to providing examples of good writing that exhibit the writing elements, traits, and applications we teach.

Bibliography

Ackerman, A. (2004, December 20). Underperforming schools—New front in today's struggle for civil rights. *San Francisco Chronicle*, p. B-7. Available: www.sfgate. com

Allington, R. L. (2001). *What really matters for struggling readers*. New York: Addison Wesley Longman.

Archer, J. (2005, March 16). Study blasts leadership preparation. *Education Week, 24*(27), 1, 18.

ASCD SmartBrief (2003, May 19). Term papers no longer a major focus [Online article]. Available: www.smartbrief.com/ascd/

Barone, M. (2004). *Hard America, soft America*. New York: Crown Forum.

Barth. R. (2002, May). The culture builder. *Educational Leadership, (59)*8, 6–11.

Barth, P., Haycock, K., Jackson, H., Mora, K., Ruiz, P., Robinson, S., & Wilkins, A. (Eds). (1999). *Dispelling the myth: High-poverty schools exceeding expectations*. Washington, DC: Education Trust.

Barzun, J. (1991). *Begin Here*. Chicago and London: University of Chicago Press.

Berliner, D. (1984). The half-full glass: A review of research on teaching. In P. Hosford (Ed.), *Using what we know about teaching* (pp. 51–77). Alexandria, VA: Association for Supervision and Curriculum Development.

Black, P., & Wiliam, D. (1998, October). Inside the black box: Raising standards through classroom assessment. *Phi Delta Kappan, 80*(2), 139–44, 146–48.

Blasé, J., & Kirby, P. C. (1992, December). The power of praise—A strategy for effective schools. *NASSP Bulletin, (76)*548, 69–77.

Botstein, L. (1997). *Jefferson's children: Education and the promise of America's culture*. New York: Doubleday.

Bradley, A. (1993, July 14). N.Y.C.'s District 2 gives top priority to educator's learning. *Education Week* online.

British Broadcasting Corporation News online (2002, November 20). Reading "can bring social change" [Online article]. Available: http://news.bbc.co.uk/1/hi/education/2494637.stm

Buckingham, M., & Coffman, C. (1999). *First, break all the rules*. New York: Simon and Schuster.

Calkins, L., Montgomery, K., & Santman, D. (with Falk, B.) (1998). *A teacher's guide to standardized reading tests: Knowledge is power.* Portsmouth, NH: Heinemann.

Campbell, P. (2005, June 15). District's two options for "assessment literacy." *Education Week, 24*(40), pp. 33–34.

Cavanagh, S. (2003, March 5). Oregon study outlines standards for college preparedness. *Education Week, 22*(25), 6.

Cavanagh, S. (2004a, January 21). Barriers to college: Lack of preparation vs. financial need. *Education Week, 23*(19), 1.

Cavanagh, S. (2004b, October 20). Students ill-prepared for college, ACT warns. *Education Week, 24*(8), 5.

Chase, K. (1998, November). The other intelligences (oy vey!) *Educational Leadership, 56*(3), 72–73.

Clarfield, M. (2004, March). The Flexner report: One that was not shelved. *Annals of Long-Term Care, 12*(3), 31–32. ISSN: 1524-7929

Collins, J. (2001a). *Good to great.* New York: Harper Business.

Collins, J. (2001b, October). Good to great. *Fast Company, 51*(1), 90–104.

Colvin, R. (2004, November 3). Climbing out of the bunker. *Education Week, (24)*10, 38, 52.

Corcoran, T., Fuhrman, S. H., & Belcher, C. L. (2001). The district role in instructional improvement. *Phi Delta Kappan, (83)*1, 78–84.

D'Angelo, F. (1980). *Process and thought in composition.* Cambridge, MA: Winthrop.

Darling-Hammond, L. (1997). *The right to learn: A blueprint for creating schools that work*. New York: Jossey-Bass.

DataWorks Assessment Newsletter. (2000, February). *(2)*1, 1–2. Fresno, CA: Dataworks Educational Research.

Delpit, L. (1995). *Other people's children.* New York: New Press.

Dombeck, K., & Herndon, S. (2004). *Critical passages: Teaching the transition to college.* New York: Teachers College Press.

DuFour, R. (1995, April). Restructuring is not enough. *Educational Leadership, 52*(7), 33–36.

DuFour, R. (2002, May). The learning-centered principal. *Educational Leadership, 59*(8), 12–15.

DuFour, R. (2004, May). What is a professional learning community? *Educational Leadership, 61*(8), 6–11.

DuFour, R. (2005, July 15). Presentation at Solution Tree PLC Institute, Stillwell, Kansas.

DuFour, R., DuFour, R., Eaker, R., & Karhanek, G. (2004). *Whatever it takes: How professional learning communities respond when kids don't learn.* Bloomington, IN: National Educational Service.

DuFour, R., & Eaker, R. (1998). *Professional learning communities at work.* Bloomington, IN: National Education Service.

Eaker, R. (2002). Cultural shifts: Transforming schools into professional learning communities. In R. Eaker, R. DuFour, & R. DuFour, *Getting started: Reculturing schools to become professional learning communities* (pp. 9–30). Bloomington, IN: National Educational Service.

Eaker, R., DuFour, R., & DuFour, R. (2002). *Getting started: Reculturing schools to become professional learning communities.* Bloomington, IN: National Educational Service.

Ede, L. (1987). *A sourcebook for basic writing teachers.* New York: Random House.

Elmore, R. F. (1999–2000, Winter). Building a new structure for school leadership. *The American Educator, 6*–13. Available: http://www.aft.org/pubs-reports/american_educator/winter99-00/

Elmore, R. F. (2000, Winter). *Building a new structure for school leadership.* Washington, DC: The Albert Shanker Institute.

Elmore, R. F. (2005, Spring). Building new knowledge: School improvement requires new knowledge, not just good will. *American Educator, 29*(1), 20–27.

Evans, R. (1996). *The human side of change.* San Francisco: Jossey-Bass.

Ferguson, R., & Mehta, J. (2004, May). An unfinished journey: The legacy of Brown and the narrowing of the achievement gap. *Phi Delta Kappan, 85*(9), 656–669.

Ferrandino, V. L., & Tirozzi, G. (2004, May 5). Wanted: A comprehensive literacy agenda preK–12. [Advertisement.] *Education Week, 23*(24), 29.

Fitzhugh, W. (2002, November). History is fun. *Education News.org, 2.* Available: http://educationnews.org

Ford, M. P., & Opitz, M. F. (2002, May). Using centers to engage children during guided reading time: Intensifying learning experiences away from the teacher. *The Reading Teacher, 55*(8), 710–717.

Fullan, M. (1996, February). Turning systemic thinking on its head. *Phi Delta Kappan, 77*(6), 420.

Fullan, M. (2000, April). The three stories of education reform. *Phi Delta Kappan, 81*(8), 581–584.

Fullan, M. (2001). *Leading in a culture of change.* San Francisco: Jossey-Bass.

Fullan, M. (2005, March 2). Tri-level development. *Education Week, 24*(25), 32–35.

Fullan, M., & Hargreaves, A. (1996). *What's worth fighting for in your school?* New York: Teachers College Press.

Fullan, M. G. (with Stiegelbauer, S.) (1991). *The new meaning of educational change.* New York: Teachers College Press.

Gervais, F. (2004, November). Remaking high school. *American School Board Journal, 191*(11), 14–19.

Gewertz, C. (2004, July 14). Chicago to "start over" with 100 small schools. *Education Week, 23*(42), 1, 21.

Gladwell, M. (2002). *Tipping point: How little things can make a big difference.* Boston: Little Brown.

Glickman, C. D. (1993). *Renewing America's schools.* Alexandria, VA: Association for Supervision and Curriculum Development.

Glickman, C. (2002). *Leadership for learning: How to help teachers succeed*. Alexandria, VA: Association for Supervision and Curriculum Development.

Goodlad, J. I. (1984). *A place called school*. New York: McGraw-Hill.

Goodlad, J. I., Klein, M. F., & Associates. (1970). *Behind the classroom door*. Worthington, OH: Charles A. Jones.

Gordon. R. (2005, June 6 and 13). Class struggle. *The New Republic*, 24–27.

Graff, G. (2003). *Clueless in academe*. New Haven and London: Yale University Press.

Guskey, T. (2003, June). What makes professional development effective? *Phi Delta Kappan, 84*(10), 748–750.

Halberstam, D. (1993). *The Fifties*. New York: Fawcett Columbine.

Hall, A. (1994, October 12). Materials from a presentation to the Amphitheater High School English Department, Tucson, Arizona.

Harrington-Lueker, D. (2002, September 16). "Crayola Curriculum" Takes Over. *USA Today*, A-13.

Harvey, S. (1998). *Non-fiction matters*. Portland, ME: Stenhouse.

Hatch, T. (2001, February 14). It takes capacity to build capacity. *Education Week, (20)*22, 44–47.

Haycock, K. (2005, June 8). Improving academic achievement and closing gaps between groups in the middle grades. Presentation given at CASE Middle Level summit. Available: www.edtrust.org

Haycock, K., & Huang, S. (2001). Are today's high school graduates ready? *Thinking K–16, 5*(1), 3–17.

Hess, F. (1999). *Bringing the social sciences alive*. Boston: Allyn and Bacon.

Hess, F. (2004). *Common sense school reform*. New York: Palgrave Macmillan.

Hess, F. M., & Kelley, A. P. (2005, Summer). The accidental principal. *Education Next, 5*(3), 35–40.

Hiebert, J., & Stigler, J. W. (2004, Fall). A world of difference: Classrooms abroad provide lesson teaching math and science. *Journal of Staff Development, 25*(4), 10–15.

Higgins L. (2002, October 18). Students in Oak Park get hooked on science. *Detroit Free Press*.

Hillocks, G. (1987, May). Synthesis of research on teaching writing. *Educational Leadership, 44*(8), 71–82.

Hofstadter, R. (1962). *Anti-intellectualism in American life*. New York: Vintage.

Jacobs, H. H. (1997). *Mapping the big picture: Integrating curriculum & assessment K–12*. Alexandria, VA: Association for Supervision and Curriculum Development.

Jones, R. (1995, April). Writing wrongs. *The Executive Educator, (17)*4, 18–24.

Joyce, B. (2004, September). How are professional learning communities created? *Phi Delta Kappan, 86*(1), 76–83.

Joyce, B., & Showers, B. (2002). *Student achievement through staff development*. Alexandria, VA: Association for Supervision and Curriculum Development.

Joyce, B., Weil, M., & Calhoun, E. (1993). *The self-renewing school*. Alexandria, VA: Association for Supervision and Curriculum Development.

Jupp, B. (2005, Winter). The uniform salary schedule: A progressive leader proposes differential pay. *Education Next, 5*(1), 10–12.

Kahlenberg, R. D. (2004, May 4). Schools of hard knocks [Online article]. *The American Prospect Online.* Available: www.prospect.org

Kameenui, E. J., & Carnine, D. W. (1998). *Effective teaching strategies that accommodate diverse learners.* Upper Saddle River, NJ: Merrill.

Kannapel, P. J., & Clements, S. K. (with Taylor, D., & Hibpshman, T.) (2005, February). *Inside the black box of high-performing high-poverty schools: A Report from the Prichard Committee for Academic Excellence.* Lexington, KY: Prichard Committee for Academic Excellence. Available: http://www.prichardcommittee.org

Katzenbach, J. R., & Smith, D. K. (1993). *The wisdom of teams.* New York: Harper Business.

Kossan, P. (2004, May 22). Phoenix school in danger of "failing." *Arizona Republic,* pp. B1–B2.

Kouzes, J. M., & Posner, B. Z. (1995). *The leadership challenge.* San Francisco: Jossey-Bass.

Kuhrt, B. L., & Farris, P. J. (1990, March). Empowering students through reading, writing, and reasoning. *Journal of Reading, 33*(6), 436–441.

Kurtz, M. (2003, March 5). Teachers' views mixed on testing [Online article]. *Boston Globe.* Available: http//:www.bc.edu/offices/pubaf/journalist/greatest/teachers

Lambert. (1998). *Building leadership capacity in schools.* Alexandria, VA: Association for Supervison and Curriculum Development.

Lasch, C. (1995). *The revolt of the elites.* New York: Norton.

Learning 24/7 (2005, April 7). *Classroom Observation Study.* Study presented at the meeting of the National Conference on Standards and Assessment in Las Vegas, Nevada.

Lewis, A. C. (1998, May). The importance of evidence. *Phi Delta Kappan, 79*(9), 643–644.

Lewis, A. C. (2002, March). School reform and professional development. *Phi Delta Kappan, 83*(7), 488–489.

Liben, D., & Liben, M. (2005, January). Learning to read in order to learn. *Phi Delta Kappan, 86*(5), 401–406.

Little, J. W. (1987). Teachers as colleagues. In V. Richardson-Koehler (Ed.), *Educator's handbook.* White Plains, NY: Longman.

Little, J. W. (1990, Summer). The persistence of privacy: Autonomy and initiative in teachers' professional relations. *Teachers College Record, 91*(4), 509–536.

Little, J. W., Gearhart, M., Curry, M., & Kafka, J. (2003, November). Looking at student work for teacher learning, teacher community, and school reform. *Phi Delta Kappan, 85*(3), 185–192.

Lortie, D. (1975). *Schoolteacher: A sociological study.* Chicago: University of Chicago Press.

Loveless, T., & DiPerna, P. (2000, November). Achievement doesn't matter in becoming a blue ribbon school [Unabridged online article]. *Education Next.* Available: http://www.educationnext.org/unabridged/20012/loveless.html

Manzo, K. K. (2003a, April 30). Panel calls for writing revolution in schools. *Education Week, 22*(33), 10.

Manzo, K. K. (2003b, October 8). Teachers picking up tools to map instructional practices. *Education Week, 23*(6), 8.

Marino, J. (1998, February). Between the lines of Goodlad, Boyer, and Sizer. *English Journal, 77*(2), 19–21.

Marshall, K. (2003, October). A principal looks back: Standards matter. *Phi Delta Kappan, 85*(2), 105–113.

Marshall, K. (2004, September 1). Let's clarify the way we use the word "curriculum" *Education Week, 24*(1), 43.

Marshall, K. (2005, June). It's time to rethink teacher supervision and evaluation. *Phi Delta Kappan, 86*(10), 727–744.

Marzano, R. J. (2003). *What works in schools: Translating research into action.* Alexandria, VA: Association for Supervision and Curriculum Development.

Marzano. R. J. (2004). *Building background knowledge for academic achievement.* Alexandria, VA: Association for Supervision and Curriculum Development.

Marzano, R. J., Pickering, D. J., & Pollock, J. E. (2001). *Classroom instruction that works.* Alexandria, VA: Association for Supervision and Curriculum Development.

Matthews, J. (2004, February 17). Seeking alternatives to standardized testing. [Interview with Deborah Meier]. *Washington Post* online: 1–10.

McLaughlin, M. W., & Talbert, J. E. (2001). *Professional communities and the work of high school teaching.* Chicago: University of Chicago Press.

Meier, D. (2002). *The power of their ideas.* Boston: Beacon Press.

Miller, M. (2003). *The two percent solution.* New York: Public Affairs.

Mintzberg, H. (1994). *The rise and fall of strategic planning.* New York: Free Press.

Mitchell, R. (2004, April 27). Dumbing down our schools. *Washington Post,* p. A21.

Mitchell, S. (August/September 2004). Reviving locally-owned retail. *Flagstaff Voice,* p. 1.

Mortimore, P., & Sammons, P. (1987, September). New evidence on effective elementary schools. *Educational Leadership, 45*(1), 4–8.

Murray, C. (2005, July 19). Reading, math up for nine-year-olds [Online article]. *eSchool News Online.* Available: www.eschoolsnews.com

National Commission on Writing. (2003, April). *The neglected "R": The need for a writing revolution.* The College Board.

Nelson, B. (1994). *1001 ways to reward employees.* New York: Workman.

New York City Leadership Academy. (2003). Advisory Board: Anthony Alvarado [Online biographical listing]. Available: http://www.nycleadershipacademy.org/01_02_03_03_member.html

Noguera, P. (2004, May). Transforming high schools. *Educational Leadership, 61*(8), 26–31.

Odden, A., & Kelley, C. (2002). *Paying teachers for what they know and do.* Thousand Oaks, CA: Corwin Press.

Odden, A., & Wallace, M. J. (2003, August 6). Leveraging teacher pay. *Education Week, 22*(43), 64.

Olson, L. (1995, February 8). Students' best writing needs work, study shows. *Education Week, 14*(20), 5.

Olson (2005, January 26). Calls for revamping high schools intensify. *Education Week, 24*(20), 1, 18–19.

Perkins-Gough, D. (2002, November). Rand report on reading comprehension. *Educational Leadership, 60*(3), 92.

Peters, T. *Thriving on chaos.* (1987). New York: Knopf.

Peterson. P. E. (2005, Spring). The children left behind. *Education Next, 5*(2), 3.

Petrides, L., & Nodine, T. (with Nguyen, L., Karaglani, A., & Gluck, R.). (2005). *Anatomy of school system improvement: Performance-driven practices in urban school districts.* San Francisco, CA: NewSchools Venture Fund.

Pfeffer, P., & Sutton, R. (2000). *The knowing-doing gap.* Boston: Harvard University Press.

Phi Delta Kappan, 86(2). (2004, October).

Popham, W. J. (2004, November). Curriculum matters. *American School Board Journal, 191*(11), 30–33.

Postman, N. (1985). *Amusing ourselves to death.* New York: Penguin.

Postman, N. (1988). *Conscientious objections.* New York: Alfred A. Knopf.

Postman, N. (1997). *The end of education.* New York: Alfred A. Knopf.

Postman, N., & Weingartner, C. (1969). *Teaching as a subversive activity.* New York: Delacorte Press.

Powell, A. G., Farrar, E., & Cohen, D. K. (1985). *The shopping mall high school.* Boston: Houghton-Mifflin.

Reeves, D. B. (2001, December). Leave me alone and let me teach! [Online article]. *The School Administrator.* Available: www.aasa.org/publications

Reeves, D. B. (2002a). *Assessing educational leaders: Evaluating performance for improved individual and organizational results.* Thousand Oaks, CA: Corwin Press.

Reeves, D. B. (2002b). *The daily disciplines of leadership: How to improve student achievement, staff motivation, and personal organization.* San Francisco: Jossey-Bass.

Richardson, J. (2002, February). No excuses for low learning. *Results* [Newsletter], pp. 1, 6. Oxford, OH: National Staff Development Council

Rose, M. (1989). *Lives on the boundary.* New York: Viking Penguin.

Rosenholtz, S. J. (1991). *Teacher's workplace: The social organization of schools.* New York: Teachers College Press.

Sanders, W. L., & Horn, S. P. (1994, October). The Tennessee Value-Added Assessment System. *Journal of Personnel Evaluation Education, 8*(3), 299–311.

Sausner, R. (2005, August). Making assessments work. *District Administration, 41*(8), 31–34.

Schaffer, R. H. (1988). *The breakthrough strategy: Using short-term success to build the high-performance organization.* New York: Harper Business.

Schmoker, M. (1999). *Results: The key to continuous school improvement.* Alexandria, VA: Association of Supervision and Curriculum Development.

Schmoker, M. (2001a, October 24). The Crayola curriculum. *Education Week, 21*(8), 42–44.

Schmoker, M. (2001b). *The results fieldbook: Practical strategies from dramatically improved schools*. Alexandria, VA: Association of Supervision and Curriculum Development.

Schmoker, M. (2002, May). The real causes of higher achievement. *SEDL Letter, 14*(2), 3–7.

Schmoker, M. (2003, February). Demystifying data analysis. *Educational Leadership, 60*(5), 22–25.

Schmoker, M. (2004, February). Tipping point: From feckless reform to substantive instructional improvement. *Phi Delta Kappan, 85*(6), 424–432.

Schmoker, M. (2005). Here and now: Improving teaching and learning. In R. DuFour, R. Eaker, & R. DuFour (Eds.), *On common ground: The power of professional learning communities* (pp. xi–xvi). Bloomington, IN: National Educational Service.

Schmoker, M., & Marzano, R. (1999, March). Realizing the promise of standards-based education. *Educational Leadership, 56*(6), 17–21.

Senge, P. (1990). *The fifth discipline: The art & practice of the learning organization*. New York: Doubleday.

Sizer, T. (1992). *Horace's school*. Boston: Houghton-Mifflin.

Sizer, T. (2003). Two reports. *Education Week, 22*(32), 25.

Smith, P. (1987). *Redeeming the time: A people's history of the 1920s and the New Deal*. New York: McGraw-Hill.

Smith, W. F., & Andrews, R. L. (1989). *Instructional leadership: How principals make difference*. Alexandria, VA: Association for Supervision and Curriculum Development.

Sparks, D. (1998, March/April). Professional development. *AEA Advocate*, 18–21.

Sparks, D. (2001a, April). The real barrier to improved professional development. *Results* [Newsletter], p. 2. Oxford, OH: National Staff Development Council.

Sparks, D. (2001b). *Conversations that matter*. Oxford, OH: National Staff Development Council.

Sparks, D. (2003a, Winter). Change agent. *Journal of Staff Development, 24*(1), 55–58.

Sparks, D. (2003b, Spring). The answer to when is now (interview with Jim Block). *Journal of Staff Development, 24*(2), 52–55.

Sparks, D. (2004, Winter). From hunger aid to school reform (interview with Jerry Sternin). *Journal of Staff Development, 25*(1), 46–51.

Sparks, D. (2005). *Leading for results*. Thousand Oaks, CA: National Staff Development Council/Corwin.

Stiggins, R. J. (1999, November). Assessment, student confidence and school success. *Phi Delta Kappan, 81*(3), 191–198.

Stiggins, R. J. (2001). *Student-involved classroom assessment* (3rd ed.). Upper Saddle River, NJ: Merrill/Prentice Hall.

Stigler, J. W., & Hiebert, J. (1999). *The teaching gap: Best ideas from the world's teachers for improving education in the classroom*. New York: Free Press.

Surowiecki, J. (2004). *The wisdom of crowds*. New York: Doubleday.

Swanson, C. B. (2004, January 28). The new math on graduation rates. *Education Week, 23*(43), 40.

Temes, P. (2001, April 4). The end of school reform. *Education Week, 20*(29), 36.

Tirozzi, G., & Ferrandino, V. (2005, March 30). Short-changing tomorrow's school leaders. *Education Week, 24*(29), 12.

Togneri, W. (2003, March). *Beyond islands of excellence: What districts can do to improve instruction and achievement in all schools—A leadership brief.* Washington, DC: The Learning First Alliance/Office of Educational Research and Improvement; U.S. Department of Education.

Tucker, P. D., & Stronge, J. H. (2005). *Linking teacher evaluation and student learning.* Alexandria, VA: Association for Supervision and Curriculum Development.

Tyack, D., & Cuban, L. (1995). *Tinkering toward Utopia.* Cambridge, MA: Harvard University Press.

Vacca, R. (2002, November). From efficient decoders to strategic readers. *Educational Leadership, 60*(3), 6–11.

Vail, K. (2001, January). Nurturing the life of the mind [Online article]. *American School Board Journal.* Available: www.asbj.com

Viadero, D. (2001). Whole-school projects show mixed results. *Education Week, 21*(10), 1.

Wagner, T. (2004, October 27). The challenge of change leadership. *Education Week, 24*(9), 40–41.

Wahlberg, H. J. (1988, March). Synthesis of research on time and learning. *Educational Leadership, 45*(6), 76–85.

Walshe, R. D. (1987, October). The learning power of writing. *English Journal, 76*(6), 22–27.

Wiggins, G. (1994). None of the above. *The Executive Educator, 16*(7), 14–18.

Wiggins, G. (1998). *Educative assessment.* San Francisco: Jossey-Bass.

Wiggins, G., & McTighe, J. (1998). *Understanding by design.* Alexandria, VA: Association for Supervision and Curriculum Development.

Wiggins, G. & McTighe, J. (2005). *Understanding by Design, 2nd edition.* Alexandria, VA: Association for Supervision and Curriculum Development.

Wise, A. (2004, September 29). Teaching teams: A 21st-century paradigm for organizing America's schools. *Education Week, 24*(5), 43.

Zakaria, F. (2004, November 1). TV, money, and "Crossfire" politics. *Newsweek,* 35.

Zinsser, W. K. (1988). *Writing to learn.* New York: Harper & Row.

Index

About the Author

Mike Schmoker is an author, speaker, and consultant living in Flagstaff, Arizona. He is a former middle and high school English teacher and central office administrator. He has written numerous articles, which have appeared in *Educational Leadership, Phi Delta Kappan, Education Week,* and *Time* Magazine. His four books include the ASCD bestseller *Results: The Key to Continuous School Improvement,* now in its second edition, and *The Results Fieldbook: Practical Strategies from Dramatically-Improved Schools.*

Contact the author at 2734 N. Carefree Circle, Flagstaff, AZ 86004. Phone: 928-522-0006. Fax: 928-522-0007. E-mail: schmoker@futureone.com

Related ASCD Resources: Improvements in Teaching and Learning

At the time of publication, the following ASCD resources were available; for the most up-to-date information about ASCD resources, go to www.ascd.org. ASCD stock numbers are noted in parentheses.

Networks

Visit the ASCD Web site (www.ascd.org) and search for "networks" for information about professional educators who have formed groups around topics like "Restructuring Schools" and "Quality Education." Look in the "Network Directory" for current facilitators' addresses and phone numbers.

Online Professional Development

Go to ASCD's home page (http://www.ascd.org) and click on Professional Development to find ASCD's online course *Creating and Sustaining Professional Learning Communities.*

Print Products

Accountability for Learning: How Teachers and School Leaders Can Take Charge by Douglas B. Reeves (#104004)

Creating Dynamic Schools Through Mentoring, Coaching, and Collaboration by Judy F. Carr, Nancy Herman, and Douglas E. Harris (#103021)

Results: The Key to Continuous School Improvement, 2nd edition, by Mike Schmoker (#199233)

The Results Fieldbook: Practical Strategies from Dramatically Improved Schools by Mike Schmoker (#101001)

School Leadership That Works: From Research to Results by Robert J. Marzano, Timothy Waters, and Brian A. McNulty (#105125)

Videotapes

What Works in Schools: School Factors with Robert J. Marzano (Tape 1; # 403048)

The Results Video Series (two tapes) with Mike Schmoker (#401261)

For more information, visit us on the World Wide Web (http://www. ascd.org), send an e-mail message to member@ascd.org, call the ASCD Service Center (1-800-933-ASCD or 703-578-9600, then press 2), send a fax to 703-575-5400, or write to Information Services, ASCD, 1703 N. Beauregard St., Alexandria, VA 22311-1714 USA.